Rassa Shastra

RASSA SHASTRA

Inayat Khan
on the
Mysteries of Love,
Sex, and Marriage

Hazrat Inayat Khan

Ibis Press
An Imprint of Nicolas-Hays, Inc.
Berwick, Maine

Published in 2003 by
Ibis Press
An Imprint of Nicolas-Hays, Inc.
P. O. Box 1126
Berwick, ME 03901-1126
www.nicolashays.com

Distributed by Red Wheel/Weiser LLC
Box 612
York Beach, ME 03901-0612
www.redwheelweiser.com

Library of Congress Cataloging-in-Publication Data
Inayat Khan, 1882-1927.
    Rassa shastra : Inayat Khan on the mysteries of love, sex, and
marriage / Hazrat Inayat Khan.
      p. cm.
    Previous edition published in 1938 under title: Rassa shastra : the
science of life's creative forces.
    ISBN 0-89254-071-0 (paper: alk. paper)
    1. Sex (Psychology) 2. Love. 3. Marriage. I. Title: Inayat Khan on
the mysteries of love, sex, and marriage. II. Title.
    BF692.I5 2003
    297.4'4--dc   212003045279

Cover design by Daniel Brockman
Printed in the United States of America
BJ
09 08 07 06 05 04 03
7   6   5   4   3   2   1

CONTENTS

I. SEX.

Sex is a direction. Two is a part of one, growing out of one. As the conductor guides the harmony, each movement of his baton demands a second movement. A single motion is not possible, a single stroke has no meaning; but as soon as there is a second motion, then begins the rhythm of the music that wins the hearts of children. In the same way every single expression of activity reveals two aspects or directions of the same action; and these may be distinguished from each other as its positive and negative aspects.

The Supreme Intelligence, which is the source of this world of variety, works through numberless paths and channels. Every channel it takes must necessarily be but a limited expression of itself, and it is humanity that has been considered by the wise of all ages as its clearest and final expression; as it is written in the Semitic tradition, Man was created last and " in His own image".

Think of human intelligence. The tendency of human intelligence is to limit. From the hosts of ideas that come to him, man must select; he can follow one path only. As he advances along his chosen path, he finds that it branches right and left; and ever and again he must make a fresh choice. His life may be called an unending choice; and his limitations make him what he is. He must choose his house and a room in his house; he attaches himself to a certain community and to a certain faith. He says, "I am a Christian; an Englishman; a Londoner; an inventor", and so on, as he comes to qualities and details which in his own opinion constitute his individual self. By his habit of mind he is inclined to begin by looking first at the smallest and most limited aspects of himself.

And how does man create his life? Firstly, he views an object; and then, inspired by that object, he moves on to further creation. He plans a picture, and as he works at it, the picture itself suggests further developments to him. He paints and looks and is pleased; and then he begins anew. Thus his intelligence works its way out. And every act of his life, as he thus works his way, shows these same two aspects or directions, one expressive, the other responsive. It is through the reciprocal action of these two factors that each activity of his advances towards perfection.

In this same way the Supreme Intelligence seems to create its design, inspired by its own activity, as is the artist by his picture; and it reveals that its very nature is such that it must forever be advancing, breaking a way and hewing out a means by which to express itself. And its every activity shows two aspects, that is to say two directions, which balance and complete each other, giving light and shade to the picture, giving rhythm to the music, developing the vision of perfection.

II. HALF-BODIES.

In Sanskrit woman is called *ardhangi,* the half-body — half of that complete body constituted of male and female. Throughout creation each element attracts to its self its like; as Sa'adi says: "Each element returns in time to the single goal of that element". This law may be more clearly observed in the attraction that exists between the sexes, and is indeed the chief reason of the attraction between these two halves which are derived from each other. Each sex is made of the element of the opposite sex; the female born of the seed of the male, and the male moulded in the womb of the female.

The harmony that exists between persons of the same sex is also accounted for by this similarity. As each element attracts to itself its own element, so male harmonizes with male, and female with female. A man feels in his own sphere when he is with his men-friends, talking and chatting freely, without conventions, formalities or restraint. So a maiden is harmonious with maidens; and a matron among matrons. But greater harmony and more naturalness is found between individuals of opposite sexes; and the reason of this lies in their contrast. Though of the same element, they are counterbalancing aspects of it; and each sex clearly perceives that each provides the other with what that other lacks. Each draws out something in the other that would otherwise be lost, and makes alive some part of the other that

3

would otherwise lie as dead. Each sex draws from the other a thoughtfulness, a consideration, the thinking nature. It is through this contrast that the loving nature in man or woman is awakened, so that the heart which was a grave of love becomes a fertile soil, where any seedling of affection will flourish, and bear flower and fruit.

The one may draw from that different other a spiritual quality, a moral quality, a talent, a merit, a virtue that had lain enclosed in a shell, as a pearl lies in the depth of the sea, to become valuable only when brought up and used. There are properties of the spirit which are in its depth, awaiting a lifting hand, and which are brought to the surface only through help coming from one of the opposite sex.

The sexes are dependent upon each other; but of the two, the male is more dependent upon the female than she is upon him. Her position in the scheme of nature is a more responsible one; and the greater the responsibility of a being, the greater is the dependence of others upon that being. An infant, whether boy or girl, is entirely dependent on the mother from the time that the seed is conceived, to the moment of its breathing the air of the earth. "The arms of the mother are the cradle of heaven", it is said, and from infancy to youth the whole attraction of the boy is towards the mother; the cases where this is not so are exceptions, where there is something different from the normal state of being.

It is the mother who keeps harmony between father and child, and between brothers and sisters. In poverty, she has the care of the money; in sickness, the burden falls upon her. She is the centre of the pain of the house. It is her part to keep the family in friendship with the world without, in sympathy with neighbours; to welcome strangers, and to receive visitors with a smile. Mohammed says, "Heaven lies at the feet of the mother". Upon her constancy and endurance depends the unity of the home, which is the unit of the state.

Sometimes we see perfection of human form or personality; and then we seem to see in the one individual something of the attributes of both sexes. A man called handsome always represents some trait of the refinement of the feminine; and in the same way a man's beautiful personality has a touch of the gentleness of the female nature. Nor can a woman's beauty, or character be finished without some of that dignity which is masculine.

III. ATTRACTION AND REPULSION.

Attraction, and equally repulsion in sex, depend upon the workings of the positive and negative forces in life. Although the male sex may generally be characterized as the positive, and the female sex as the negative force in humanity, yet this characteriation does not necessarily hold good in all planes of existence. It can easily be seen that when a positive power is confronted by a power that resembles itself, but is positive to a still greater degree, it becomes negative; as a talkative person becomes a listener in the presence of one more talkative than himself. In the same way a negative power ceases to be negative, but becomes positive, in the presence of a power that is similar to, or still more negative than itself.

The positive is expressive, whilst the negative is responsive, — as speaking is positive, while listening is negative. Throughout life these two forces are seen balancing and completing each other: in the swing of the pendulum; in the beat of the conductor's baton, as it marks the rhythm of the music.

Since each finds its completion in the other, these two forces exercise an attraction upon each other. By the very nature of things, the negative cannot but be attracted by its positive aspect; and the positive is inevitably attracted towards its negative aspect. The positive is indeed the first to feel attraction; for it is always seeking scope for expression,

6

and reaching out towards that in which it finds its balance; and it finds in the negative that pliability for which it searches, with the whole strength of its being, in its demand for response. The negative therefore represents beauty, while the positive represents power. For power is not of itself beautiful. Power is attracted towards beauty; its desire may be called beauty; and again its power becomes powerless before beauty.

The moon balances the power of the sun. If it were not for the moon, the sun would burst into flames, and set the whole universe on fire. If it were not for the moon, the worlds would break in pieces, and the cosmos would scatter.

The negative, by providing the necessary balance to the whole being of the positive, gives beauty to its activity. On the other hand, the positive gives strength to the negative. By its expression of itself, the positive may be said even to create the negative. It is this which is symbolically expressed, when it is said that Eve was created from the rib of Adam; that is, the negative created from the positive and actually part of the positive. The negative, then, is derived from the positive and is strengthened by it; and it has its return thither again. For the positive indeed draws from the negative its positive character. The existence of each depends thus entirely upon the other; and every purpose of each, even its ultimate purpose, is accomplished in the co-operation of both.

Repulsion is caused either through lack of power or of scope, on the part of positive or negative. When the positive has not the power to draw to itself the negative, it draws it perhaps half-way, or a little more or less; a lack of power that may actually repel the negative. Or else the positive, being first attracted

7

to the negative, and then feeling itself too weak, recoils. Or again the positive may be slow to express itself; and remaining in the attitude of the negative, it provokes confusion, since the negative finds no channel in which to respond.

Again the negative, in responding, may express itself in the manner of the positive, and then there must result a clash or conflict; for then there is no scope for the positive. Or else the positive, expressing itself with intensity, may drive back the negative. Or the positive may find the response of the negative so narrow, that it finds itself deprived of sufficient opportunity for its full expression. In such cases harmony is not possible, because the negative does not furnish sufficient opportunity, or scope, for the positive.

Inharmony therefore results when one or the other is frustrated in the desire for self-expression. But harmony is more natural than inharmony. The union of male and female should provide an opportunity within that union, for each to attain the fullest expression of which each is capable; or that neither shall find within it an obstacle which impedes his or her fullest development. Every soul is indeed seeking for completion — a search that too often ends in the destruction of beauty, since the human being, deluded and ensnared by the life on the surface, forgets to look into his self, and to discover what is the nature of that 'I', which so desperately desires satisfaction.

8

IV. ON SOME IDEALS.

The man who has never had an ideal may hope to find one; he is in a better case than the man who allows the circumstances of life to break his ideal. To fall beneath one's ideal is to lose one's track of life; then confusion rises in the mind, and that light which one should hold high becomes covered and obscured, so that it cannot shine out to clear one's path.

The fall of Napoleon may be dated from the day that he abandoned Josephine. With the breaking of the ideal, the whole life cracks and dissolves. As soon as a man begins to think, "I have done wrong by such and such a person, or such and such a principle", he ceases to be a king within, and cannot be a king without. This does not mean to say that the good succeed in life and that the evil fail, but rather that man progresses alone through sincerity to his ideals. For the good of each man is indeed peculiar to himself.

Religion is the school that has developed man; and the ideals that religion presents form a path that leads upward to perfection — that innate and yearning desire of every soul. The difficulty arises when man sees his principles as his goal, and not simply as a means to his goal; for when he begins to worship his own principles, he becomes a simple idolater, and he destroys the essence and the life of his ideal.

Can anyone point to a date in history when man first gained wisdom? Wisdom is the property of humanity. The expressions of this wisdom differ at different times, to suit different peoples; and it is the differences that have always been noticed, and and do not the similarities.

Artist or workman, philosopher or scientist, wherever found, arrive by their individual paths at the same knowledge of the laws of nature, and thus learn those fundamental laws of ethics, which do not change from country to country, nor from age to age, nor contradict each other.

And the wise of all ages have taught that it is the knowledge of the divine being that is life, and the only reality. Although a human activity may consist of a number of complicated motives, some of which are base and gross, it is the aspiration towards divinity, the desire towards beauty, which is its soul, its life, its reality. And it is in proportion to the degree of the strength or weakness of his aspiration towards beauty, that man's ideal is great or small, and his religion great or small.

There exists an affinity between the negative and positive which inclines the one towards the other; and towards the union which results in a fresh conception of beauty. Ancient mythology has beautifully expressed this in the figure of Cupid, whose wings show that he is a spirit, and who, coming in the guise of a child, represents childhood. Cupid, the spirit of affinity, draws two of the opposite sexes together, for the purpose of a birth of beauty. Thus it happens that human kind is strongly attracted to its opposite; and when the expressive and responsive tendencies of both awaken through love and passion, a third being is created, and a ray finds its abode in the mother's womb.

Thus it is seen that it is the spirit that possesses

the sexes, to attract them together for its own purpose of manifestation. Therefore many religions and philosophies have considered the sex-relationship to be most sacred; since it is thus that the spirit manifests itself. And for the same reason the sex-relationship may become the most sinful, if this purpose of the spirit is lost to view.

For to disregard this purpose of the spirit is a defiance of the law of the whole mechanism, such as inevitably drags the structure to ruins.

There is nothing of this earth more valuable than the seed of man, the source of further manifestation; and by its loss every door of happiness in life is closed. But man is usually so careful with his money and properties and jewels, and desires so earnestly to increase them, that he sacrifices everything to them; and he becomes regardless of the jewel of life which is his own life, character, and personality, and which is more precious than any property.

Again, every religion prohibits marriage between blood relations, the rules varying somewhat; as for instance, in some Western countries, marriage between an uncle and his niece is permitted — an union usually considered unlawful in the East, as in some other Western countries. It is now said, however, that certain modern social revolutionaries are questioning the laws which make blood-relationship a bar to marriage. These laws are, nevertheless, rooted in truth; for where there is no expansion, there is no progress.

Expansion is necessary for physical reasons. Between blood relations the negative and positive forces are not contrary enough; and when the battery which depends upon the strength and contrast of these forces becomes weaker, its issue becomes correspondingly weaker; or else there is no issue. Morally also, progress demands expansion. Has not the whole of creation been gradually built by expansion?

The vigour of the Western nations is, to a great extent, due to the intermixture of innumerable tribes and races. Even now, before our eyes, a young and promising nation of extraordinary vitality is developing in the United States of America, formed of the many elements of all the European nations. There are certainly disadvantages in inter-racial and inter-national marriages; but these are small in comparison to the advantages.

Pride of birth and of rank, and also of community and religion, have always kept humanity back by forming barriers that prevent natural expansion. The Western aristocracies have suffered incalculable loss thereby; but this is most clearly seen in the history of the East, where the Hindu castes, by limiting themselves within their own circle, have brought ruin to their race. The Eastern custom of child-marriage is a product of pride of family, since each family has wished that the wife of their son should be brought up in the traditions of their own family. The conservative ideas of the Parsees, that most exclusive community, operating through many generations, have produced notable physical alterations in their people, among whom, to instance one point, only a small percentage have normal eyesight.

The national ideal which unites human beings in a desire to uphold certain social laws and certain ideals of civilisation, is necessary to human life; but to make these ideals barriers that separate humanity into distinct sections must effectively prevent the progress of humanity as one whole; and this progress is the basic idea of religion.

Nations endeavour to progress as nations, and races as races; and each race and nation is prepared to hinder the progress of any other. Thus, through wars and conflicts of every kind, the patriotism of each race has become so individual and distinct, that an inter-racial marriage means that one or other of the contracting parties must renounce his or her patriotism; a renunciation that is sometimes almost a death.

It is the young people who are most often drawn to an inter-racial marriage, the young, generous, and idealistic. But it is not often that they meet their corresponding social class; it is not often that aristocratic or educated aliens meet the aristocratic or educated natives of any country; and yet it is true that there is a great similarity between the corresponding social and intellectual classes of all civilisations.

People marry for various reasons: some because it is the custom, some for the sake of home life, because man is a dependent creature, and desires a companion in the joy and sorrow of life, or because marriage carries a weight in the social world; for generally it is a home where a couple live in a house. Others again are tempted by rank, birth, position, wealth; and these marry the thing desired, and not the human being. Others have a wish to leave children, so that their name may not pass from the earth, or the property they have collected fall into the hands of strangers; and some other few marry for love.

There is a tendency in husband and wife to own his or her mate; and the stronger of the two will often attempt to do this by the right of marriage itself, having forgotten the reason for which he or she contracted the marriage. This tendency of ownership makes many a marriage a captivity.

Zafar wrote: "O Zafar, you cannot call him a man, though he be in human form, who is without thought in anger or counsel in passion". The human being is supposed to take counsel with his own principles of modesty, of chivalry, and of shame; and therein to differ from the animals; and that expression of his sexual passion which has no regard for these principles may be called adultery. Adultery is, in fact, that which, done under a spell of passion and in the blindness of the moment, brings afterwards repentance and shame, with remorse for the consequences. A drunken man does in his intoxication what he would never have done when sober; and so laws are framed to control drunken madness and folly.

To resist evil, however, usually means to participate in and be guilty of the same evil. There is a story told of Mohammed, that a man who had always maligned him and behaved as a bitter and treacherous enemy came to see him, and his disciples, hoping for revenge, were disappointed and indignant to find that Mohammed treated his despicable enemy with courtesy, even deference, granting his request. "Did you not see the gray in his beard?" asked Mohammed after the man had gone. "The man is old, and his age at least called for my courtesy." It is forgiveness and that forbearance which is a recognition of the freedom and dignity of the human being, that consume all ugliness, and burning up all unworthiness, leave only beauty there.

V. TYPES OF LOVERS.

In this world of variety no two faces are alike, nor any two characters, nor any two personalities. In all ages it has been the belief of the wise, and the realization of the greatest intelligences, that there is unity in the scheme of things; and that harmony rules the whole of existence, which proves its evolution from one single source of activity. And that the Source from which all springs is a distinct and definite individuality, is proved by the distinct individuality of each created thing. In each, one sees 'I', conscious of its separate, distinct, and peculiar identity.

No two roses, even of the same stem, are exactly alike; no two leaves are identical. And the wider our study into human character, the stronger grows the conviction that each human individual is remote, unexplored, and unknown. Nevertheless, just as we call a whole variety of flowers by the name of rose, so we may vaguely generalize and divide human beings into varieties, distinguishable from each other in their general attitude towards the opposite sex.

We see the idealist — imaginative, a worshipper of beauty — whose heart is touched by one of the opposite sex who appeals to his idealism, lose himself in his thought of her. The beauty that he sees before him is the food of his love; on this beauty his love is sustained; but so soon as his heart is deprived of it, then his love weakens. And when his ideal ceases to be ideal in his eyes, then his heart dies.

We see also the artist in love, a man of wit and intelligence, refined and fastidious, but affectionate too, and with intense sensibilities that respond instantly to beauty. Fine and yet gross, he is quick to love and yet able to hide his affection; he is ready to be kind to her who loves him, and to conceal his attraction from her who attracts him most. The artist in love is attracted by beauty and grace; and according to his evolution, and the manners of his environment, he is interested in all that appears to him exquisite, lovely in manners, in form or in speech.

Then we see a third type, who is fond of women without seeing much difference, or specifying which is which. On whatever woman his glance falls, he sees her nude. In loving a woman, he does not love the human being, but simply the woman. His emotions are dead; he is uninterested in her; he finds her simply a means for his own self-expression.

A fourth type is rough and brutal. If he thinks of a woman, it is to enjoy her in thought. He is crude in his actions towards women, passionate, lustful. He is not only uninterested and regardless of her feelings, but he does not stop at actively inflicting suffering, so long as he finds his own satisfaction.

And we see yet another type of man, who perhaps alone should be called lover; a man not susceptible, though kindly and sympathetic to all. But once he loves, he is ready to accept poison or nectar at the hands of his beloved; and once he professes his love to his beloved, he is absolutely hers. A man who keeps his love constant upon his beloved, and holding her in his heart, cannot admit any other save her alone. Whilst the idealist is captivated by the beauty of personality, this lover looks at the beauty of his beloved's soul. His love is as sacred to him as his religion; she whom he loves is a part of his own being; and in her life he lives. Love is to him an everlasting bond here and in the hereafter; it is the best proof to him of persistence of life after death.

2.

There was an idea of old amongst the Hindus that mankind falls into three distinct classes: *Deva*, the divine man, *Manusha*, the human man, and *Rakshasa*, the monster man. Before marriage it was the custom, and it still exists, to consult someone who could read the horoscopes of the contracting parties, so that a third person, an intelligent observer, could give advice, and thus prevent the union of two beings belonging to distinct types of humanity, such as never could be harmonious to each other.

The idea was that there should be harmony between two: both *Deva*, or both *Rakshasa;* thus kind to kind, wise to wise, cruel to cruel, foolish to foolish. While it was thought there should be harmony between mates of classes near to each other — that is to say between *Deva*, divine-man, and *Manusha*, human-maid; or between *Manusha* and *Rakshasa* — it was believed there was little chance of harmony between *Deva* and *Rakshasa*, that is between divine and monster-man; and that either the finer nature would be dragged down and ruined by the grosser, or else the grosser nature would be destroyed by the finer nature. The third person, the Brahmin, under the excuse of reading the horoscopes, when he could make every enquiry about character, was able to place the man and woman in their rightful categories as he observed them; and thus to give warning, and possibly avert future disaster.

VI. THE CHARACTER OF THE BELOVED.

I.

In Persian poetry a certain character, called *shukhi*, is given to the beloved woman. The charm which the Persian poet describes by *shukhi* is more usually found in woman than in man; although it is possible that many women would consider it a characteristic of a man towards the woman who loves him. This character of the beloved can scarcely be called beautiful, although it is alluring. Its chief property is heedlessness, or a kind and careless independence that is touched with insolence.

Changeable, she shows and yet she does not show herself; quick to laugh, she is quick to seize upon the amusing or ridiculous side of things; and yet she herself is sensitive to ridicule and to attentions; trying very daintily to test just how deep her lover's feeling for her has gone.

Selfish and amiable, she responds and yet refuses to respond; light-hearted and talkative, mocking and perpetually amused, though ready to take offence, she is a constant source of surprise to her lover, who feels he must ever be on the alert, if he would really hold her; and too, that he must move gently, lest he should injure a being that seems to him so much gayer and lighter, so much weaker and slighter, so much more delicate, and airy, and graceful, than he knows himself to be.

This beloved is life to her lover; and therein, in truth, lies the secret of her attraction for him. She is always fluttering outside the reach of his comprehension. Her sunshine and laughter invigorate; her mockery and ridicule, her thousand demands are incentives; even her light-hearted insolence is a spur to prompt him to efforts in all kinds of directions, where otherwise he would never have ventured.

But what reason does he give to himself for his love? He will give a hundred reasons, and yet be puzzled to give even one that is sufficient. He despairs of making her understand the depth of his feeling; he imagines himself ill and dying, and her answer when the news is brought to her:

> She lightly laughed; 'And so is Mazhar dead?
> 'Alas, poor helpless one! I knew not, I,
> What was his trouble.' Then again she said:
> I did not think him ill enough to die.'

Or the lover imagines himself dead, and in his grave; and he pictures her, as she lightly steps over the grass that covers him, drawing her draperies closely round her, lest perchance he should stretch up his hand and touch them. And yet love, like the fire, dies out unless it is fed with fuel; and the lover in his despair recognises this too, and blames her for giving the encouragement that he desires. She represents in herself evanescence of joy, the swift passing of laughter, the difficulty of holding the moment of beauty.

> The heart's unending malady is she,
> And she herself the only remedy.

According to Hindu ideas there are four different types of women, who influence the lives of men.

Padmani, the ideal of the poet, fine, and delicate, and graceful in bearing, is made to be loved, and is herself full of love. Her voice is low and soft, her words are gracious, her expression is sweet and gentle; she is admired by women, and her friendship and presence bring heaven on earth to men. When she makes a friend of a man, it is something of a venture or step, as it were, taken out of her own circle; for women are her natural friends, and to them she turns, both out of interest and for protection. In her heart is kept one beloved alone, whom nothing can remove. Her smile for him is as the unveiling of heaven; her kind glance is a lasting impression; her sweet words ring for ever in his heart. And it is clear to all that she looks on him as her king.

She is intelligent and simple, courageous and shy, patient and enduring, constant and firm in thought; and she is moved by all things that are tender and appealing. There is a fittingness in her behaviour. She has a love of order, a respect for the aged, patience and constancy before difficulty; and she is self-denying and unassuming throughout all. Her affections are deep, and she finds them inexpressible; but her face, her features, her glance, every word and every movement show a picture of beauty and devotion to the ideal. Rarely does one see a *Padmani* in life; and the man who wins her heart gains the kingdom of Indra-Loka, the heaven of the Hindus.

Chitrani is beautiful and brilliant. She is happy amongst women, but prefers the friendship of the opposite sex. She is affectionate by nature, and desires affection. Her voice is music, a song; and there is poetry in her words. She is not so idealistic as *Padmani*, but she is refined and skilled in manner, and delightful and amusing in expressing her likes and dislikes. She herself loves but one man, though her manner may show another that he might perhaps be able to win her love too. She is vain and she is modest; she is bold and she is exclusive. She plays at hide-and-seek with her lover. Her swift glance, the lift of her eyebrows, her slightest gesture, a movement of a hand or of a shoulder, will convey her thought or mood as no words can. She expresses her love and wins her lover's heart a thousand times over; and one straight look of her eyes draws his soul to the surface. She is controlled by him, and yet controls. She is with him and yet apart. She is Maya, the elusive one. She is the pearl of his heart.

Shankani is strong, rough and determined. She is desperate in her likes and dislikes. Her heart is gained in a moment, if her passion is touched; and she changes easily from one lover to another. Men are her preoccupation; but the love of any one man does not impress her deeply, nor could she for her part hold any man for ever. She is forward in expressing herself, and she is emotional. She is little inclined for friendship with women, and they find her inconsiderate towards them. She is ungainly in figure. She is unbalanced in mind. One day she will esteem a person highly, the next day her devotion is thrown to the ground like a stone, and broken.

Hastani is greedy and impulsive. Voice, movement, words, all show that self-indulgence and passion predominate in her. She does not form any deep or serious attachment in life; and she will suddenly break a thread which unites, with a word of anger, or a hasty feeling of displeasure or disagreement. Her actions are untimely; there is an abruptness in her ways that jars peace or friendship. She does not appeal to women, who are on their guard against her and fear her; nor does she prove a pleasant and lasting comrade, even to her own mate.

From the conception of the ideal of *Padmani* to the idea of *Hastani*, there is seen an increasing force in the power of expressing emotion, but also a lessening in the capability of holding any lasting attachment. In *Chitrani* there is perhaps an equal balance between depth of feeling, and beauty in expression of feeling; while in *Padmani* there is found an absorption in the ideal which means selflessness. And this is actually more fruitful in producing the beauty that gives solace and calm and the glow of happiness, than anything else in life.

VII. MODESTY.

Haya, that is to say modesty, is not artificial in the sense, for instance, in which obedience to many of the laws framed as a means of regulating the community may be called artificial. Just as wisdom and morality are learned of nature, so also does modesty come from nature. It is a quality of beauty. It is the essential quality of beauty which the great artist understands who, by veiling his thought, conveys an impression many times more beautiful than does the artist who is unskilled in expression.

The poet dives into life, listening to that voice which is inaudible to those engaged on its surface. Not only poets sound the depths, for all men strive for beauty, which lies at the bottom of each man's spirit. But if any, after sounding the depth of life, have been able to convey something of their exaltation and their anguish at the touch of beauty, it has been the poets, with their veils and clouds of language.

Consciousness in fact demands a veil. God and man are the two aspects of being, and man and woman are the two aspects of humanity, and a covering envelops that phase of each aspect where consciousness is most developed; in other words, the highest phase of each aspect of life is covered and veiled. Communion with God, the revelation of man's unity with God, and his recognition of God,

24

have always been expressed in parables. Christ, like every great mystic, conveyed the beauty of his teaching in veiled words. Religious language has always been symbolic; truth has ever been given under symbols, such as that of gods and goddesses, and the symbol of the cross.

For every tendency of man, nature seems to make a corresponding provision; it is this that reveals the intelligence working behind this world of names and forms. No man-made moral dictates modesty; it is the nature of beauty to veil and guard itself, and disclose itself but little. And very different customs in different races show this quality, but become hardened and rigid in its external expressions in social life.

In America, a country of greater freedom than any other, of vast spaces and wide horizons, where men from all parts and of every class gather in the hope of finding larger opportunities and more liberal chances for self-expression, this same quality is seen prevailing unweakened. Natural human characteristics in fact become stronger under freedom. Natural tendencies develop into customs, which grow rigid and lifeless in time, and losing their meaning become in their turn fetters upon the freedom of the very nature that produced them.

In some parts of the East, women of society and education dressed for social occasions veil themselves entirely, and out of modesty leave only the feet uncovered; whilst others clothe the feet and the whole body except part at the sides of the waist — customs that would seem offensive to women of the same position and distinction in Western countries, who through modesty cover all except shoulders, neck and arms. Though these customs differ, all

25

express the same tendency to modesty. A custom in a race called primitive by European society demands that a man shall not look at the mother of his bride; out of respect for her he must not raise his eyes to her face. It is as if dignity veiled the face of the older woman from his gaze. And this custom seems but an extreme form of that feeling which in countries far remote from this race demands that the bride herself shall appear veiled at the marriage ceremony.

The emotions which the human being, conscious of the beauty of humanity, veils in himself, he also desires to cover in others. It is this desire that the Prophet Mohammed described as the true religion, *al haya wal iman.* The veil of the widow is a covering of her sorrow from the gaze of the curious, but it is equally a warning sign to the stranger to avert his eyes and thus shield her; the same may be said of the veil of the nun. The desire to hide emotion, which is one of the highest attributes of humanity, cannot exist without a tendency to shield another. It is this shielding tendency which is the source of courtesy, — courtesy which ennobles and exalts mankind, beautifying the relationship of the sexes towards one another and of class towards class.

To violate modesty is to develop coarseness which breaks the ideal of humanity. But by preserving this inner restraining grace man develops his perception of ideal beauty; and 'poor in spirit', he is indeed blessed, for he becomes conscious in human life of heavenly loveliness.

2.

In the veiling and unveiling of beauty lies every purpose of creation. The Shah of Persia, who loved the beautiful Princess Zeb-un-Nissa for the thoughts
26

she disclosed in her verses, once wrote to her: "Though I bear your image in my mind, I would never permit my eyes to raise themselves to your face". At another time he wrote asking her, "What sort of love is yours that you do not unveil your beauty to me?" She answered, referring to the tale of Majnun and Leila, who are the Romeo and Juliet of the East, "Though my heart is the heart of Majnun, yet I am of the sex of Leila; and though my sighs are deep, *haya* is a chain upon my feet". The fame of her learning and beauty spread far and wide, but Zeb-un-Nissa never married. A poet, a philosopher, she lived absorbed in her own meditations and studies. She never saw her lover, although for long they exchanged verses in an intellectual interchange of thoughts on life, truth and beauty.

After many years, he wrote in passionate longing to her, that if he could see her but once, it would be to him a sacred vision; and in answer she sent a poem that said:

> The nightingale would forget his song to the rose,
> If he saw Me walking in the garden.
> If the Brahmin saw My face,
> He would forget his idol.
> Whoever would find Me,
> Must look in My words;
> For I am hidden in My words,
> As the perfume in the petals of the flowers.

Thus she replied to his desire to see a sacred vision, describing the Divine Veiling of the Divine Presence. Even in this way have all those who touched the Divine Life and caught sight of the Divine Beauty spoken of their inspirations. Remember the words of Krishna who said, "Whenever religion (*dharma*) is threatened, then am I born."

In the veiling and unveiling of beauty lies every purpose of creation. The lover is first of all dependent upon seeing his beloved and upon her response to him. But there comes an evolution in his love that changes his whole outlook; and then his love rises above such earthly needs, and becomes independent and strong of itself. It is this independence that makes love secure and that shields love in the face of *haya*, the very defence of beauty. Love, grown thus strong and independent, becomes that inviolable loyalty to the ideal and that indestructible constancy which Zeb-un-Nissa thinks of when she sings:

> If the beloved face thou canst not see
>   Within thy heart still cherish thy desire;
> And if her love she will not grant to thee,
>   In thy love never tire.
>
> Although her face be hidden from thy sight,
>   Within the sanctuary of thine heart
> Still keep her image for thy own delight,
>   Hidden apart.
>
> And if the Keeper of the Garden close
>   Before your face the inexorable gate,
> O linger yet! The perfume of the rose
>   Will float to you, and find you as you wait
>   Not all disconsolate.

(Songs of India.)

VIII. THE AWAKENING OF YOUTH.

The Eastern poetic idea defines several stages in the approach of youth to maturity. In the first awakening of a liking, a fondness, a tenderness for one who is not of her sex, the girl is pictured as not thinking at all of expressing her feeling, but as trying to cover it, even from own consciousness. If there is a load of pain, she may let escape one cry. If there is a great admiration in her heart, the trembling of her lips say more than any word she utters. In the presence of her lover she is speechless, and the expression of her emotion reaches as far as her throat, to be instantly driven back into her heart again. The lowering of her eyes at the sight of her lover is the only sign that she consciously gives of her love, and though her face may light up, she draws back her hand if he touches it, or would wish it to remain in his. She turns away her face if he offers a kiss, and her confusion when embraced tells her youth.

And then comes a mysterious and exquisite time, which gives promise of that faithfulness from which springs the fulfilment of life. Then, with one direct look she expresses what a hundred of her words could not explain; and shy — though most shy when some other besides her lover is present — her gentle response to his advances would move the dwellers in heaven. She gives freedom to her feelings and yet with reserve, with shyness she yields and yet does not yield. She carries the thought of her lover in her heart day and night; when she is alone she is content to give herself up wholly to her interest in him. But since she does not feel clearly whether in doing this she does wrong or not, or should blame herself or not, she fights against such thoughts, without banishing them, all the time that the duties of the day keep her under the eyes of others. She tells even her closest companion and friend but little of her love, for she would hide it even after it is apparent to all. The grace of her perplexity is winning, and with it she fans the fire in the heart of her lover.

Then follows a full awakening; and her glance fallen on her lover is as an arrow; it pierces through his heart. Her kiss thrills him to the depth of his being, and her embrace holds intense joy for him. She is frank, sincere, and open; courageously she responds to him, desiring even to express her own emotions, as she gallantly faces the truth she has discovered. And thus comes the culmination of youth, where abides the fulfilment of love.

The development is undoubtedly the same in the youth of both sexes, but for various reasons it cannot be so distinctly traced in the growth of the boy's character. Moreover, it is the mind of the maiden that has been the poet's central theme and that has captivated his interest. There is something besides beauty, there is something more than a charming loveliness in the sight of youth that carries in the heart a tender place; and whether the beholder actually knows of the tenderness that youth feels or not, he cannot fail to see some effect of it. For love, like a flame, cannot fail to give out light.

And with the birth of a response to the fascination

of the opposite sex comes the dawn of that ideal for the sake of which creation exists, and of that hope towards which the whole of creation is irresistibly drawn. As the Hindustani poet expresses it: "It was the desire of finding an ideal love which brought me here upon earth; and this same desire of attaining the ideal is now taking me back whence I came".

IX. COURTSHIP.

I.

Courtship is the foundation upon which married life is erected. Real courtship is in all love that is directed towards an object with the hope of gaining it, and with constancy in the pursuit of it. Belief that the object will be attained some day, and confidence that the desire to attain will not weaken before it is fulfilled, is of the spirit of true courtship.

One sees many cases where a young man or girl, out of a desire to get all the pleasure possible, is happy with one friend in one season, and with the change of season changes the friend, — a kind of restlessness that may increase to such an extent that youth, making merry, may seek a new companion or new face with whom to share every fresh enjoyment. Such as these know only of pleasures that pass, and remain in the same place where they were. And those who seek to recall the first spring-time of emotion in many experiences, and so go from one love-affair to another until they grow to be more interested in change than in anything else, lose sight of the real beauty of courtship and its real joy. Their loves that change so often make but little difference to them, and their hearts that have suffered no wound, since love has never really touched them, remain unilluminated.

Then too often one sees that a young man or

woman, out of great cautiousness perhaps, or a fundamental lack of confidence or trust, will have several love-affairs at a time, thinking to choose at last the one that may seem closest to his or her ideal. Although this may prove a successful way up to a point, it is certainly one that will prevent ultimate success in life. For love is the power that is the original cause of Creation; it is the battery working behind the mechanism of the universe; and this original power is lamed in the individual, when he attempts to divide it by directing it towards the more than one, who are held in his view as possible objects of his love.

As to the effect of indecision upon others, change-ableness on the part of a man seems usually to have more harmful results than changeableness on the part of a woman. Since a woman's position in life is the more delicate one, whether regarded from the moral, or social, or physical point of view, there is more danger that the injury that a man inflicts upon her may prove irreparable. At the same time, a woman is perhaps to be more censured than a man if she proves fickle and changeable, since she naturally possesses greater stability, more especially in an affair of the heart.

The man or woman who, out of cautiousness or for whatever reason, has more than one in view in courtship, is not able to give enough to any one, or take enough from him; he is unable to take for the very reason that he is unable to give. Think then what he loses. If he were able to see those ocean waves that move in his heart — the heart that is vaster than any sea — he would never be deluded into thinking that any price could be too great to pay for the loss of that emotion which comes in the intensity of love.

The right mate comes at the right time, and then indeed all cautious testings seem useless, crackling like straw.

As soon as feeling is divided for the sake of any such reason as the testing of the beloved, it becomes a business, — one can no longer speak of it as love. And as soon as one's feeling is divided for such a reason, one begins to develop deception, and the emotions eventually become obscured by deception. There cannot, indeed, be any sincere love without single-mindedness, nor any fragrant love without sincerity.

A tendency is often seen in young people of wishing to arouse jealousy and of attempting to gain a deeper affection by showing the lover how much others admire them, and therefore how worthy of admiration they are. But it is the wrong tactics, for the current that should flow in a single stream is of necessity disturbed by such a manœuvre. A persistent lover will no doubt fight his battle on love's field, to overcome his real or supposed rival; but after winning the battle the current of his love must be weakened and may be exhausted; usually indeed, on account of the conflict and strain sustained, it becomes so attenuated that at any moment the thread can break or wear through.

One also sees young people viewing courtship from a practical standpoint, thinking what practical benefit they may derive. Whether it is money, or comfort, or position they think of, it is the thing they are looking for that they love, and not the person. However loving or affectionate a couple may appear, there can only result disappointment for one of them if their courtship is built on such a basis. For by an inner law of nature, if one of two friends is disappointed, the other cannot be entirely happy.

When the stream of love flows in its full strength it purifies all that stands in its course, as the Ganges, in the teachings of the ancients, purifies all who plunge into its sacred waters. It is more than a wonder, more than interesting or beautiful, to see the devotion of youth in the presence of the beloved. The pain of his longing in her absence, his effort to come to her, and his planning to communicate with her when there is no channel or means, and his imaginations, — what he would like to tell her, how he would like to put it, — all are washed away in that present moment when he is face to face with her.

Sincere courtship is in itself a religion. Surely no religion can teach more than love can. When the beloved becomes so much the centre of life that the lover begins to lose his selfishness through thought for her; when he is so impressed by her beauty that no other beauty, no matter how great, can make him falter in his allegiance to her; when for her sake he becomes gentle and considerate; when he confesses to her what he would not have any one know on earth; when his desires turn towards honesty and sincerity in all things through his honesty and sincerity in love, — is there not then something in his life greater than the religion that is merely taught? Has he not himself received a direct inspiration from heaven above? A lover, thus inspired, looks forward with the same hope to his future life with the beloved, as the pious do to life in the hereafter. The meeting between two such lovers is nothing less than a divine communion, since God Who is love, and was asleep in their hearts, is now awakened within them.

Many say, and rightly, that parents should have control in the love affairs of their children, for whose sake they have borne so many troubles and difficulties. And who could enumerate the sacrifices that parents willingly undergo to support their children and to protect them from all hardship? It is undoubtedly hard for any to find that the child who was once so helpless and dependent is no sooner grown than he wishes to take a step quite independently of anyone, — and a step that will influence his whole future happiness. Besides, as they say in the East, youth is blind, and especially blind when love rises in the heart, covering reason with clouds of emotions, and sweeping away discretion in a storm of feeling. At such a moment it is a third person who can judge of the real state of affairs. Shall the place of this third person be denied to the parents who, in the majority of cases, live their youthful lives again in the youth of their children?

At the same time, parents who separate their child from the beloved, whether by force or by influence, are in danger either of driving the child who is courageous and independent, away from them altogether, or of crushing the heart of the weak one in such a way as to leave a pain there that is never forgotten. Many a girl comes in her disappointment to look upon her parents, once her friends, as her bitterest enemies. Parents and children live in such different worlds; the temperament, the outlook of the old is so strange to the young.

And is it really possible for any one being to take over the responsibility of the life of another? Can it really be thought that any soul has the right to control another soul by power or force? There is one control: affection, which is the only legitimate deterrent; but affection loses all happiness once it disregards freedom. Freedom of the self and freedom of the loved one, — true affection can never lose sight of either. And whether it be through love of mother or father, or of the one who loves in courtship, once the freedom of the beloved has been hindered, a fault against love has been committed. Where the attentions of love are not acceptable they should be withdrawn; where the lover finds that the beloved is troubled by the expression of his love, or that the heart of the beloved is changed and bent in a new direction, so that his power is no longer able to keep it in the direction that he wishes, then instead of causing harm to the beloved, let the lover (whether father, or mother, or whoever it be) cease to demand a response. He may perhaps become indifferent and erase his love; if so, good. But the real lover accepts the bowl of bitterness from the hands of the beloved as a draught that purifies and strengthens for life, knowing that crucifixion alone is the source of resurrection.

X. CHIVALRY.

There is a story told of Sa'adi, that chivalrous and most ideal of poets, that he loved a girl very dearly, and admired and valued her so greatly that he prized her more than all else in his life, so that there was nothing that he would not do for her sake. One day coming to see her, he found her, though he could scarcely believe his eyes, in the arms of another; but going away quietly again, he took his stand at the gateway of her house. When the other man saw Sa'adi standing there, he thought, "Surely now, filled with jealousy, he is waiting to kill me". But Sa'adi, as he saw him approach, called: "Friend, be at peace. I am waiting to give you a word of sense; that as I have seen and gone away quietly, so do you, if you should see her in the arms of another. For that is the way in which the wise love."

Gairat, or chivalry, so often takes the form of jealousy that the one is usually confounded with the other. This same male tendency lies at the root of duelling, a custom not foreign to any part of the world, which down the ages has been the cause of every kind of conflict and upheaval. The honour of one may be the honour of another, or of ten, or a hundred others; and thus a woman's honour may be upheld as that of a king.

Man has always held woman as most sacred in

life, as more precious to him and as appealing more to him than the rest of life. If she be his mother, he sees her as his source and creator, his only sustainer and protection; in heartbreak and disappointment, and in the very depths of despair comes the thought of the mother, who was his first friend before anyone was attracted to him, and his first guardian and teacher. If she be his sister, he thinks more of her than of himself, for her position in life is more delicate than his; she is the honour of his family, and he considers that he shares the responsibility of his parents for her. None of this goodness is artificial; it is of the very essence of humanity, springing from the nature of things. To a father the responsibility of a daughter seems greater than that of a son; her dishonour or unhappiness strikes at him most keenly. And in that closest relationship of life, a word against his wife destroys his happiness and peace; he would accept any degradation to shield her; and this equally if he be attached to a woman worthy of ideal, or to a prostitute, to one who has lost all sense of self-respect. In each relationship her honour is his own honour.

This male tendency is seen taking selfish and brutal forms in the social life of the community. For instance, when the consciousness of the responsibility that the birth of a daughter places upon the family, has induced such a custom as the killing of female children at birth, — a custom found in many different countries at different times; as now, in Western civilisation, even among the well-to-do or wealthy, parents restrict their families, and take means to prevent the birth of any child, male or female, through dread of responsibility. Or again, the natural dependence of woman is often greatly increased by man; for so strong is the feeling that a man's responsibilities in life are greater than hers, — since he bears hers as well as his own, — that woman is deprived in order that he may the better have every advantage that offers. In order that he may be better fitted for his fight in the world, her natural disabilities are added to and increased.

One sees in the West that girls often receive less opportunities for education than their brothers; that daughters inherit a less portion than sons; that the work of women is paid at a lower rate than that of men. And in the East, this male tendency is responsible for such customs as the seclusion of women. Thus everywhere, East or West, even if unexpressed, there exists this tendency to regard the position of a woman as the honour and care of a man, and as consequently less dependent upon her own efforts than upon his.

It is the thought of individual freedom that is attacking the old ideals, and destroying also this ideal of *gairat*, or chivalry; for in spite of the selfish, even brutal forms that it may take, it is an ideal; and he who follows it possesses a religion. In the West, man is found accepting greater advantages of life without accepting corresponding responsibilities. The Hindu, with a less strong thought of individual liberty, still preserves many ancient ideals; and no student of Hindu life can deny that these are as sacred to him as his worship of gods and goddesses, and are part of his *dharma*, or religion. If the Hindu once calls a woman sister, or daughter, or mother, he regards her as such all his life, through the sacred bond of his promise; and feels in honour bound to protect and sustain her, though she may not be related to him in any way.

40

There is a feminine chivalry which the poets of
Hindustan call *naz*, a beauty that shines out if
lighted by the deference of a man. It is a beauty
that lies silent and hidden, till an act of attention, of
admiration, or respect on the part of a man stimulates
the vanity in which it is rooted. Under courtesy and
consideration, it unfolds to a perfection that shows
in the woman's every action and feeling; in her
words and deeds, smiles and tears, so that every one
of them becomes filled with beauty. The value that
a woman sees in a man's small acts of courtesy is
rarely understood by man, and it seems to him
inexplicable and part of that mystery which he
believes shrouds her from him. But there is no
woman, of no matter what type or class, country or
nation, in whom there is not this beauty, which the
courtesy of man alone discloses.

There is another kind of feminine chivalry which
the poets call *nayaz*. This tendency is seen expressing
itself in the gallant and courageous response that a
woman will make to her admirer; or it may express
itself in a gentle, yielding forbearance towards him.
It makes her lenient and forgiving to a man, modest
and gracious. When he has a desire to protect her
and to help her, it is a gentle chivalry on her part
that makes her put herself, as it were, into his hands.
She gives him that trust, which he wants her to place
in him, and accepts his attentions, just because he
so desires her to trust him and to receive his care
or homage. It is her chivalry which constrains her
to value male chivalry and hold it precious.

And there is yet another kind of feminine chivalry:
nakhra, which is the radiance and beauty that man

recognises as feminine. When a woman possesses this quality, nothing can hide it; it shines out unwavering and undimmed, natural, without self-consciousness. No effort on man's part is needed to disclose it; nor on the other hand is it the result of any conscious effort of her own. There is in it no pointing with a dart, no aiming with an arrow, towards some target of admiration or reward. It lies in her simple and unaffected recognition of a certain part of life as her kingdom, over which she is by right the queen, and where she reigns, with a consideration towards those dependent upon her, that is the very essence of aristocracy and chivalry.

No situation in life can extinguish this natural beauty; and it may be seen shining in the unconscious movements, in the unclouded gaiety and sunniness, and in the intelligence of a maiden, who is as yet untouched by any burden of life. It is a queenliness, a womanliness that irradiates its possessor at every step of her journey through life; and more than any other human quality, it wins the heart of man.

XI. MARRIAGE.

I.

Marriage is from nature, and is simply an attachment, Some minds see a great significance in marriage, believing that couples are born and made for each other. Others believe that this attachment is but the outcome of contact, arising from the nearness of two individuals to each other, which, developing, leads them to form a partnership. Actually one sees marriages which illustrate both these ideas. The first may be seen operating in the vegetable kingdom; it may be traced in the disposition of two leaves on the same stem, one balancing the other and responding to the other. The second may be seen ruling in the animal world, where mates become attached to each other through propinquity, until something comes to disturb their lives together, and then, absent from one another, they forget each other and readily accept a new mate.

But man has always something of sincerity and faithfulness in his nature. Though he lives his life in a changing scene he values steadiness and constancy; the origin of his soul is indeed that One and Eternal Spirit, which does not change. And it is this human tendency to constancy that has helped to bring about the recognition of the attachment between man and woman, a recognition that has developed into many and varied institutions of marriage. For the human pair, so attached, have wished to think of themselves as united with a desire for constancy; and they have also wished others to look upon them as a couple joined in a constant partnership.

The idea that an individual man or woman has been created the one for the other is found among all races at all times. It rests on common human experience. One often sees an individual, possessed of a desire to marry, who makes many friends without becoming attached to anyone; it seems as if he were groping towards his own mate, destined for him, and that he cannot rest until he finds her. And again one sees two who have met many without forming any real attachment, who instantly upon meeting feel united, as if they had been made for each other.

One sees that all creation is aiming at perfection. Every atom is working to fit into its proper place; and either it attracts or else it is attracted to the fulfilment of that perfection, which is the reason for its existence. All the different particles of an object are in time brought together; no matter how scattered, eventually they meet; this is the secret underlying existence. And the coming together of a man and woman who see their attachment to each other as something sacred as religion, is true union; the hope with which they look forward that their partnership may endure in unbroken constancy makes theirs a real marriage; and in this ideal is found the perfection of human life.

But this natural, sacred union is influenced from both sides in the modern state: on the one side by the Church, and on the other side by the law. Marriage has degenerated into a business affair, advertised on all sides as subservient to ideas of material profit and advantage. It is even suggested now that an external

44

authority shall decide whether a couple be physically fitted to marry, so that the liberty to make even this decision may be taken out of their own hands.

And once they are bound together, the laws of the Church keep a couple bound together whether the attachment proves to be real and sincere or not, making them captives for life; so that often the promise taken in the Church service is the only tie that remains, and it becomes a lock that secures the imprisonment of two lives. Having no joy in their union a couple, mutually willing to part, may be thus debarred from experiencing the joy of a real marriage within their Church. And the social law stands ready to enforce captivity and to inflict punishment should they break their imprisonment; and thus prevents them from following that sacred path of real attachment which leads to perfection of life. For marriage is neither a religious ritual nor a business contract, though the attitude of the Church makes it appear as the one, and the State as the latter.

The free-thinker, revolted by the purely formal marriage, goes to the opposite extreme, advocating what he calls free love. This ideal of free love, by which man and woman have entire freedom in marriage and divorce, without reference to Church or State, will be practicable and possible when all the children of the community are equally under the care of the whole community. Nevertheless, for the individual to have this freedom without a spiritual ideal of life would prove a curse. And it must now be acknowledged that the world, which is progressing in many directions, is weakening in others; and every day shows a weakening in the regard for purely spiritual ideas, such as are necessary in the democracy taught by the greatest teachers of humanity.

If the spirit of freedom becomes destructive it loses the essence of democracy. The true democrat says, "There is no-one to whom I, in my humanity, will yield as to a superior"; but he also says, "there is no-one among humanity whom I dare despise or injure". Until that far-off day arrives, when freedom exists everywhere alike for the strong or the weak, untainted by any spirit of intolerance, there must be safeguards to ensure order in the community. Until that day, marriage, or the formal recognition of the human attachment, will be necessary, not only in order that the interests of the children may be safeguarded, but so that woman, who has not in the East or West of the world that recognition which makes her socially as independent as her mate, and whose position in life from every point of view is consequently a more delicate one than his, shall not suffer unjustly.

2.

A Turkish father heard that his son was continually absent on long visits to a country place, and ordered him to give up these journeys and to remain strictly at his studies. He was a man of influence and position, and his son, from fear of him, fell in with his wishes. But later, hearing that his son had involved himself in an affair with a woman in that country place, the father sent him back to her, saying, "How otherwise shall I feel secure that my own daughter will meet with honesty and sincerity?" Here there was no covering up of the truth for material convenience, although it would have been certainly easier to repudiate the woman, and to make a virtue out of convenience; and no insincere adherence to an

46

external standard of morality, nor any dishonest attempt to enforce an ideal of monogamy upon a mind incapable of sustaining it.

The English law of breach of promise was framed to protect women; but does any one really imagine that there are now in England, owing to this law, fewer tragedies of the kind where innocent and sincere women have been betrayed? The really sincere woman is silent before treachery of this kind as before death, feeling herself to be in the presence of something before which she is powerless.

The average man is apt to look with awe upon the social laws which govern his community, as if these laws were of divine ordinance. He forgets that they are simply means devised for the most part by the average among his fellow-men, to keep order; and that they can often be traced to a materialistic point of view, directly opposite to the divine spirit of the teacher whom he professes to follow as his religious lord and guide.

Every individual has a certain motive in his life. The higher his motive, the greater the current of thought or feeling that streams from him towards it. If two mates are drawn by the same motive, they advance through life together; but if it is not so, then life may be as a swimming against the tide for each of them.

Before marriage it is hope that keeps love alive. Acquaintance, friendship, courtship are deepening stages through which hope leads the human being to that partnership called marriage. After marriage, life's progress may become difficult, unless life presents a new scope and a new avenue for hope. Hope may centre round the children; and yet that is not enough. There must be some incentive to stimulate each partner to progress along the path of life, and this is best given by each to the other, when a common interest makes them share both joy and sorrow together, their gaze centred on the same aim.

Where there is no common interest, or aim, or ambition, harmony may still exist if each has an ideal of his responsibilities to the other as a human being; it is indeed through the lack of this ideal that life breaks into pieces. And it is truly noble on the part of a couple, who through miseries and difficulties always have regard to the sacredness of the tie that connects them.

Nature is such that no two things are created alike; and the human being cannot expect his or her mate, whom nature made, to be as docile and flexible as that creature whom his imagination alone conceives. To make a friend, forgiveness is required which burns up all things, leaving only beauty; while to destroy friendship is easy.

XII. BEAUTY.

I.

It is said that in the East woman has been dominated by man; but from the Eastern point of view she can never be dominated by him. She is not only the ideal of nature's beauty, she is also the guardian of human beauty. And she has therefore been considered in the East as one enshrined, and worthy to be guarded from the strife of the world, which man, more roughly made, can more easily bear.

Regarding the most responsible purpose of her life, Zoroastrians, Brahmins and many sects of Hindus have from of old apportioned regular days of rest, even from household duties, for servants and mistress alike. And there is a widespread belief in the East that if an expectant mother comes to see many different types of faces, sometimes degrading and ugly, and to deal with many natures, the cruel, the unkind, the bitter, that the desired image, designed by nature's pen in her womb, must be disturbed and altered. Therefore she is guarded with care that endeavours to shelter her from every ugliness, and to surround her only with sympathy, gentleness and beauty. It is true that this ideal of consideration does develop into many tyrannies and fettering superstitions; but in Eastern eyes these tyrannies do not seem so hypocritical or hard as those to be seen in modern Europe, where woman with seeming personal freedom fights equally with men in the open market of life, and yet always unequally, hampered still by artificial handicaps invented by him.

Man all the world over has a desire to be the first to possess the woman who is to be the mother of his children; and this desire is rooted in the belief that the image and personality of the first man by whom a woman conceives will perhaps reflect itself in all her children; this is really a belief in the power of mental impressions, though perhaps not always consciously held. Breeders of animals in all countries point to cases in support of the idea that if a female is mated with a male of inferior breed, or one with a peculiarity, there can be no certainty that her offspring by other sires will not be tainted by the inferiority of the first mate. These beliefs and instances point to the fact that the female conceives mentally as well as physically, and that a strong mental impression may well prove indelible.

And though the modern scientific view denies that mental impressions and emotions have much effect upon the physical body, pointing, for instance, to the malformation of a head or skull, and giving this as the reason of defective mentality or of insanity, the Eastern philosopher will still ask, which defect showed itself first: was it the mental or the physical defect?

The history and the resulting psychology of every people are so different, that it is impossible for one race to see or judge the evolved customs of another from their own point of view. Man sometimes points with surprise to the deep tenderness and admiration for woman, to the despair at her loss, and to sentiments of the most beautiful loyalty to the beloved, which inspire the songs of even the wilder and less literary peoples of the world; a surprise that itself occasions surprise.

The Hindu worships Krishna by the side of his consort, and admires most of all that ideal of care and consideration of which we have spoken. The follower of Islam points to facts, such as that every woman in Islam retains her own name after marriage, which shows that she stands as a responsible individual both in the home and without. He will remember also that the Prophet always upheld the ideal of womanhood, making his followers swear, in their oath of allegiance to him, to speak no evil of woman; and asking women themselves to show dignity by their clothing and manner. He who felt so keenly the degeneration of his people, first struck in his campaign for reform at the degradation to which the brutality of men subjects woman. And the follower of Islam reflects also on the long gallery of women who would surely have fallen victims to superstition for their unusual talents, and been killed as 'witches' or 'servants of the devil', had they lived in the same periods in Christian countries, but who shine like stars in the annals of the history of Islam on account of their intellectual accomplishments or spiritual attainment. Each country defends its own ideal of woman as being the highest; and to each country there belong its peculiar tyrannies, which are but different aspects of the same blind tendencies of humanity.

There is a story told in the East, how a king was debating with his philosophers and friends upon the question wherein lies beauty. As they were talking together on the terrace of the palace they watched where below, in the courtyard, their children were playing. Suddenly the king called to the slave of the courtyard and said, handing him a jewelled cap, "Now take this and put it on the head of the child whose beauty seems to you to suit it best; choose and crown the most beautiful of all those playing down there". The slave, a little embarrassed, but pleased and interested, took the jewelled cap most carefully. First he tried it on the king's son; he saw that it suited the handsome lad and yet, somehow, the slave was not quite satisfied; there seemed to him something lacking about the child and he tried it on the head of another, and another, till at last he put it on his own little son. There he saw that the cap fitted his child exactly; it became him wonderfully; it was just the right cap for him. So the slave took his son by the hand, and leading him to the king, and trembling a little with fear said: "Sir, of the children, I find that the crown suits this one best of all. Indeed if I tell the truth, I must say this, though I am ashamed if I appear bold; for indeed the boy is the son of my most unworthy self." Then the king, and those with him, laughed very heartily as he thanked the slave, and rewarded him with the same cap for his child, and said, "Certainly you have told me what I wished to know; it is the heart that perceives beauty". For the son of this negro slave was indeed a very ugly child, as the king and all those with him saw at a glance.

Ideals are made by the diverse imaginations of men, and therefore ideals differ; but to hold the ideal is the work of the heart — that unchanging heart which contains reason, and is greater than reason, even as a hand is greater than one of its fingers.

2.

The Venus of Milo, that statue whose beauty crosses the boundaries of nations, compelling the

52

admiration of totally different schools of art, suggests that the beauty of woman conquers without arms.

There is nothing for which a man will sacrifice his all so blindly, as for the woman he loves. He can be seen discarding his standard of thought and understanding, his family and friends, his position, for the sake of her whom he loves. And one feels that Adam must gladly have left Paradise, if Eve but smiled and said it was her pleasure to walk on earth.

Woman's beauty touches man more than all other beauty. The colours, the delicacy and fragrance of flowers, the radiance and light of jewels, are but a background for her. It seems to him that all nature was created preparatory to her being. And he finds no subject so beautiful for his art, as a beautiful rendering of the two youthful figures, male and female, of humanity.

But how shall he describe her whom he loves? When he is conscious of beauty, it is then he closes his lips.

As the ocean cannot be emptied into a vessel made by human hands, so beauty cannot be captured within the limits of human definitions. There is the beauty of the pine tree, a beauty of straightness and uprightness; and again there is the beauty of the sweeping branches of the willow. Or again a curve, added to the beauty of steadiness of form, sometimes doubles that loveliness. What can explain this diversity? Beauty of movement, of gesture, of feature, of expression, of voice, — all escape explanation, which is indeed but a limited thing.

How calmly the mountains and hills seem to be waiting for some day that is to come; if you go near to them and listen, they seem to tell you this. How eagerly the trees and plants seem to be expecting some day, some hour; the hour that shall be the fulfilment of their desire. The same desire is still seen intense and pronounced in birds and in animals; but its fulfilment is in man. The aspiration which, working through all aspects of life, has brought forward such varying fruits, culminates in humanity, and prepares through humanity a path that reaches up to the height called divinity, which is even the perfection of beauty.

XIII. PASSION.

When one considers the nature of passion, one sees that it is life itself; it is energy taking substantial form and expressing itself through different channels and outlets. Different desires such as speaking, singing, dancing, laughing, crying, fighting, wrestling, boxing, are different expressions of the same energy, whose central, or final expression takes place in the passion between the sexes.

Passion is seen in the groups made by speaker and listener, or thinker and receiver, or actor and spectator, but it appears most vital and strong in the love of the lover and the response of the beloved. The passion of the poet is in his poetry; the passion of the musician composes melody; the passion of the actor declaims his part. The act of creation, in no matter what aspect, is the play of passion, whose source and root is love alone; for as man without humanity is empty, and as the body without spirit is dead, so passion without love is energy that is devoid of beauty and blind.

Passion is the desire of love. Passion is the expression of love and it is the satisfaction of love. It is no exaggeration to say that passion is the end of love; for the purpose of love is fulfilled by passion. Man's life is composed of many lives, and the circle of each is completed when the passion that inspires each is satisfied.

All things in life have a purpose; the purpose of

some is known, and of others unknown. And beyond life and beneath life exists that activity which the limited mind cannot comprehend. But so far as human understanding can probe, it can discover nothing of greater purpose and value to the world than passion. Under that covering is hidden the hand of the creator. In all aspects of life, through the animal kingdom to humanity, it is the only source and cause of generation; and that of itself discloses to the thinker its importance. The great teachers of humanity have therefore wished man to look upon every expression of passion as sacred; and as most sacred of all, that passion which exists in the love of the sexes for each other. The desire to make sex-passion a most sacred thing is seen in the teaching of Shiva; and the origin of phallic worship lay in the desire to raise in the sight of humanity the sacredness of passion, and to free it from the shame and contempt with which men viewed it.

The inclination of the ear to hear clearly shows itself when one is unable to listen owing to a disturbing noise. Then the passion of hearing is not satisfied and man becomes confused; he will beg others to keep quiet a moment, or, if weak, he will lose his temper if he is not allowed to listen to what he wishes to hear at the moment. When one smells a thing, there comes a desire to smell it until one knows what it is, until one can fully understand and appreciate the smell. And so with taste also; the taste of a delicious dish tempts man at once to taste more, to enjoy it fully. The sight of beauty gives man desire to see into its depths, until sight is satisfied. In the average man the passion of touch is, however, the most intense form of sense; for through this sense, consciousness comes to the surface. The comfort of soft clothing, of easy chairs, of warmth in winter, of coolness in summer, of the freshness of the bath, is conveyed to a man through his sense of touch. Indeed, most of his pleasures are dependent upon his recognition of touch. And this sense reaches its culmination in the passion of the body for one of the opposite sex. But it is not only the sense of touch that is energized to its very centre in sex-passion, but every sense is awake, and therefore it is that sex-passion moves mankind more than anything else in the world.

In each different aspect of joy a different plane of existence is reached, but in sex-passion all planes of existence are in motion. When accumulated energy is expressed in the abstract through feeling, it comes as laughter or tears, anger, affection, fear, or sympathy. Energy expressed through the mind comes as speech or thought; and expressed through the body as action. But the expression of intense affection towards the opposite sex brings the whole being to the surface. Consciousness which in other experiences becomes but partially external, remaining mostly within, is in sex-passion alone brought entirely to the surface. It is therefore that spiritually-minded people have abstained from sex-passion; and that religious people have considered it degrading; for the soul consciousness is thus brought without, instead of being preserved within; and the soul is thus brought to earth, although its destination is, so to speak, in heaven.

But if this world is the work of a creator, it has been created so that the Creator might experience external life. In other words the knowing aspect of life has wished to know the knowable part of life; and its joy depended upon knowing, which comes alone through experience. Moreover its evolution and

57

development depend on the inspiration which is brought by experience alone. And inasmuch as it is necessary for the knowing aspect of life, or the soul, to return at length to its original state of being, even so it is necessary for it to experience, first of all, the life it created, for the very reason that it might know.

XIV. CELIBACY.

I.

In all ages celibacy has been a religious and mystical ideal, and for two principal reasons. The first is that although the soul, born into the world, is led further astray by every fresh experience that it meets with in life, nevertheless it is sex-passion that causes the greatest delusion of all. The myth of Adam and Eve illustrates this truth; for whether it was a means taken by God or by Satan, it was at the hands of Eve that Adam ate the forbidden fruit, and not through any direct command or prompting that he himself received. And since man's final goal is the attainment of spiritual life, — his life here on earth having been all in vain if he fails to achieve it, — every effort has been made by religion to draw him away from that passion of sex towards which he is led by nature, and thus away from the greatest peril that his soul can encounter on its earthly journey.

And then again, whilst every expression of life, speech, laughter, tears, robs man of some part of his fund of energy, it is sex-passion that makes the greatest demand of all; and therefore the idea of celibacy was presented, so that man might the better preserve his energy to pursue with singleness of view that final goal of spiritual attainment.

Losses such as dimness of reason, weakness of thought, loss of memory, despair, depression, result when the inner being of man is starved, because energy has been expended, and because there is no knowledge or skill in strengthening and sustaining the inner existence. At every moment of life, and with every breath, the human being gives out and takes in energy; and whenever he gives out more than he takes in, he draws death nearer. But if energy is denied an outlet, it can be raised and used to sustain the mind and the inner being. For this reason mystics have often practised seclusion, silence, and other forms of abstinence, to preserve energy for the sustenance of the inner life; and they have found that celibacy was the most effectual means of all upon this path. "It is the spirit that quickeneth; the flesh profiteth nothing".

But man's life can never be complete without woman, and this is the error that lies at the root of the ideal of celibacy. Man's life is incomplete without woman, whether one considers his social or his political life; and no less true is this, if one considers his religious and his spiritual life. Without the sympathy of Christ for Mary Magdalene, and the nearness of the friendship of Christ to Martha and her sister Mary, the beautiful picture of the Master's life would be incomplete. Among the Prophets of the Semitic races, from Abraham down through the ages, there was always a woman to complete the course of their holy lives; and the great Hindu teachers from Brahma to Krishna are glorified together with their consorts.

Religious man, wherever found and whatever teacher he followed, has nevertheless been prone to look at contact with woman with contempt; with the thought of there being something unholy in the passionate love of woman. Indeed it is a question whether the libertine has actually debased woman as much as the religious man, who with contempt believes that to hold himself aloof from any woman and to strangle his love within him, will be for his own spiritual benefit. And is it possible to debase woman and the position of woman in the scheme of life without debasing man, and the whole of life?

In the evolution of the ego, there is undoubtedly a development towards celibacy, but this same development undoubtedly carries an increasing regard for woman, and the whole plan of life. Oriental philosophy, in discussing the ego, distinguishes between the *nufs amara* and the *nufs lawama*. The former is the individual whose whole existence is on the surface, engaged in the satisfaction of his senses, in eating, drinking, in amusements, and in sexual indulgence; and the *nufs lawama* is the individual whose physical greed is controlled by intelligence, to the extent of making him discriminate between his pleasures. The *nufs lawama* rejects those desires and enjoyments that fall below the certain standard of taste which his intelligence sets for him.

The *nufs mutmaina* represents a third and higher stage of development, in which the senses are under the control of mind. In this stage of evolution a man is absorbed in some ideal, or devoted to the achievement of some object in life, outside of self, — art, invention, trade, and so on, — and directs his energies into one channel. In his sexual passion he may be compared to the deer that comes to drink from the pool of fresh water, lying hidden in the depth of the forest, pure and untroubled; to be frightened away, by the least flutter of reflected shade, that distracts or disturbs his attention. For him, passion only exists when he loves; he cannot

61

feel passionate when he does not love. Here at last is found the admiration of woman, the beginning of love, and the real lover. What do the *nufs amara* or *lawama* know, who think of love as a pleasure?

The furthest stage in development is the *nufs salima*, in which man's consciousness is removed to an abstract plane. In the heart of a man at this point of evolution, love is raised from admiration to worship; his love is part of his being, and his passion, which is never expressed except in the intensity of love, may be compared to the alighting of a bird on earth to pick up a grain of corn. This man lives on a higher plane of life, judging by different standards; though his inspiration springs from the common life of existence. Thinker, visionary, or man of action, he becomes absorbed in the contemplation of the essence of things. He alone becomes unable to regard anything as common or unclean; although in his contemplation of the mystery of life, and in his devotion to the pursuit of truth, and his self-sacrifice to the cause of humanity, he may become gradually etherealized above every material object. Having reached this point, he is truly justified, if he should strike the path of celibacy.

2.

The story of Princess Mira Bai is the story of a *nufs salima* united to a *nufs amara*. Mira Bai was married to the Rajah of Udaipur, but soon her tastes in life developed very differently to his. He, always given up to pleasures of hunting and shooting, to the giving of great entertainments, to shows of dancing and acting, began shortly after his marriage to be irritated and vexed by the attitude of Mira Bai towards his amusements. For she was not really interested in any of these things, and gradually ceased to show any delight in them; and her mind began to be attracted to quite other aspects of life, — to considering the lot of her servants, and of the poor in the kingdom, and to philosophy and poetry. At last the Rajah, in unreasonable anger at her growing absorption in thoughts and questions that were foreign to his nature, refused to see her or to treat her with the dignity due to her in his court. Mira Bai took these insults calmly and patiently, with her accustomed sweetness and gentleness, and withdrew to a temple where she began to devote herself entirely to the study of philosophy and religion, and to the care of the poor and unfortunate.

The beauty of her hymns of praise, the music of the poetry that she composed and sang in her worship of the Divine became gradually famed throughout the kingdom of Udaipur; and on account of her great piety and learning, many were drawn to the temple where she dwelt. At length her fame reached the court of the Emperor Akbar; and he, entirely won by the thoughts and the sweet verses of her songs that were repeated to him, decided that he himself would make a pilgrimage to see her. And so, in the guise of beggars, he set out with Tansen, the divinely-inspired musician, learned in the mystery of sound, as was Orpheus of the Greeks.

After they had entered the temple, unknown to anyone, and had heard Mira Bai, so moved were they by her music and poetry that Akbər, with gratitude and veneration, presented to her a most precious necklace; and this necklace Mira Bai took and hung round the neck of the idol of Krishna in the temple, regarded by her as the symbol of the Most Divine.

63

After that the precious necklace was seen by everyone in the temple; and gradually it became clear that it was Akbar himself who had given it. When the Rajah of Udaipur heard of this visit and this gift, he felt deeply insulted, and in great anger ordered Mira Bai to leave his kingdom. So she left the temple and his kingdom, and went to Dwarka, where she spent the remainder of her life in seclusion; and from there her fame spread to the boundaries of the Empire, and her hymns became loved and were sung, not only by her own people, but by all the peoples of India.

It is difficult to translate the lyric sweetness of her verse; and the following version of one of her songs does not attempt to do more than give its substance:

My Beloved is One alone;
Everywhere, my eyes see Him only.

In search of love, I came to this world;
But after seeing the world I wept;
For I felt coldness on all sides,
And I cried out in despair, 'Must I too
    become cold?'

And with tears, tears, tears,
I nurtured that plant of tenderness
Which I had almost lost within my heart.

Putting reason in the churn of love,
I churned and churned.
Then I took the butter for myself;
Now, let him who likes take that milk.
For I have attained what I so desired,
I have found my hope.

No longer do I need your philosophies and faiths;
Nothing to me your theories and creeds;
For I have my Beloved.

He, upon whose head the crown of the universe
   is set,
Is my Beloved.
Krishna is my Lord;
To Him, I am faithful;
Let happen what happens!

My Beloved is One alone;
Save Him, I know none.

XV. MONOGAMY.

I.

Any study of psychology shows that success and happiness in life is found in singleness of mind. To focus itself, the mind takes a single direction; and singleness of view cannot fail to develop singleness of purpose. Many are the paths that lead to success; the difficulty lies in keeping strictly to the chosen path, or in other words, in retaining singleness of mind. There is one means only by which man can attain to a realization of the religious ideal of the Godhead, and that is through sincerity and single-mindedness in the conduct of everyday life.

So it is that the ideal of monogamy has been considered by the wise as no less sacred than religion. In this ideal is found verily the natural law of religion.

Even among polygamous peoples, monogamy prevails; because the one who is bound to several in marriage is most often devoted to one alone, and thus monogamy is, in a sense, more natural than polygamy. It is a tendency that is seen to a certain extent in birds and beasts. Doves, for instance, when mated, remain attached to each other and share equally the responsibility of rearing their young. Deer and other herbivorous animals always keep to one mate, and only after long separation, when they have lost consciousness of each other, will they accept a second mate. Such loyalty among animals is always a

66

source of interest to man, and is in itself significant.

Once, in India, a man out hunting killed a bird, and saw, as it fell to the ground, that its mate flew down seeking after it; and when he came near to take his prey, he found the mate dead beside it. So impressed was he by the sight of the lifeless body, lying beside its slaughtered mate, that he never thereafter went shooting. Constancy never fails to impress by its beauty.

In testing gold, we recognize the real gold by its enduring qualities. The real gold lasts; and what the human being calls divine in character, is something that is enduring in its beauty, and thus different, distinct, and apart from the world, which is ever changing.

The value of the things of life lies in the worth that man attaches to them; of themselves they have no value. There is a time when toys are treasures; but the child who cries for a toy comes to an age when he gives it away. And at every step in a man's evolution the values of power, and position, and wealth change in his eyes. And so, as he evolves, there arises in him a spirit of renunciation which may be called the Spirit of God. Gradually he recognizes the real value of those fair and lovely qualities of the spirit that change not. In the ideal of monogamy, in the ideal of devotion to one alone, abides a recognition of loyalty and constancy, as being the most valuable, as being the divine attribute of man.

To the poet, to the artist, whatever be his art, to the idealist, the idea of the one Beloved is part of his being. With a selfless sincerity he is faithful to his vision of beauty; and every thought that tempts him from his loyalty to her is to him a going astray. No social law or moral teaching is needed to chain

67

him to his beloved; his inward impulse keeps him to her.

It has been no uncommon thing to find in any age, in any country, cases where a bereaved mate has been unable to live on after the death of the beloved. Most often one sees the bereaved one of a true union living a dead life, suffering a long drawn-out crucifixion, till death terminates the enforced separation. Amongst the Hindus, that most idealistic of races, marriage gives a sacred position to the wife, so that she is, ideally, entirely dependent upon her husband to fight every battle of life for her, and to them the thought that a wife could marry a second time seems intolerable. Such stories of fidelity became honoured to an extent amongst the Hindus as to make *sati* a custom, and it became customary for Hindu women to imitate in their own lives stories of great devotion, and by dying on their husband's grave, to give thus the greatest proof of affection.

2.

There is a story told about the wife of Jayadev, the poet of the Sanscrit age, whose *Ashtapadis* have been sung for centuries with unbroken interest. The story tells that Jayadev's wife visited the Court of the Queen to offer sympathy according to custom, after the Queen's sister had died in *sati*. Jayadev's wife remained silent before the Queen, who began to feel insulted that she did not express admiration for the great ideal that her sister had shown, or condole with her for her own loss. "Does it not seem to you a great and noble proof of love?" asked the Queen. "Indeed, yes . . ." answered Jayadev's wife, but she seemed to hesitate as if she had no words and the Queen kept this in her mind.

68

Some time later the Rajah happened to be away with Jayadev on a tiger-hunt; and the Queen sent word to his wife to say that the poet had died on the expedition. "What?" said she, "Is Jayadev dead?"; and she sank unconscious, and never recovering consciousness thus died.

For a youth to prefer death to dishonour is a great and generous ideal, but when this ideal becomes a custom, then the ideal has become an idol. It seems more terrible than the custom of *sati* that a young man should kill himself for an ideal at the very threshold of life. But indeed, that the human being should hold life cheap in comparison to his ideal has nothing of terror or horror in it; the horror begins when custom enforces such a sacrifice upon the individual who cannot understand, or willingly accept it.

The joy of devotion to one alone, the joy, that is, of loving someone so much as to feel entirely loyal and true, is such that it cannot be compared in its fulness to any other in life. It is a joy that cannot be known except to the pious in the path of love. The virtue of this plant of truth and constancy reared in the heart, spreads through its branches into each part of life in ever-springing virtues that are constantly blossoming and bearing the fruits of every happiness and blessing.

There is a verse of Hafiz which says, "My heart is so pure in its love for you, that indeed it shows no purity; for save you, it loves no-one". The apparent confusion of this thought lies in this: that to love sincerely one cannot love more than one; and yet love must grow, for to cease to grow means but to wither and to die.

And to love one alone, and that one truly, is to

69

respond and to expand to all the beauty of life. The real lover laughs at him who says, "I have loved, but my beloved failed me and therefore I love no more". The real lover, like Aladdin, has his magic light, and he creates his vision of beauty. The real lover cries like Majnun, "To see the beloved, you must have my eyes". He says, "O you who blame, you who despair, and you who hate, cannot see".

An English poet, writing of the sun, has said:

> When the sun begins to spread his rays,
> He shows his face ten thousand ways;
> Ten thousand things do then begin,
> To show the life that they are in.

and the poet Shams'tabriz has written:

> When the sun showed his face
> Then appeared the faces of the forms of all worlds;
> His beauty showed their beauty;
> In his brightness they shone out;
> So, by his rays, we saw, and knew, and named them.

A frame of pure and sincere love is as a torch upon the path of the lover. It reveals to him the mysteries of life, as it wakens the answering gleam of light, the soul, in each created thing.

XVI. POLYGAMY.

I.

Monogamy and polygamy depend upon temperament. A monogamous temperament could never be otherwise than monogamous. And there are temperaments that will always have a tendency towards polygamy; no matter how happily placed in life, or how carefully guarded, these naturally seek variety of experience in sex.

In the lower animal creation, the polygamous temperament is seen predominant. There one male has a number of females. And one male is capable of procreation through a number of females, and in this latter respect man is no exception.

To permit polygamy is simply to recognise a natural human tendency with frankness. But to permit polygamy does not in any way mean the same as to enjoin polygamy. Mohammed, for instance, advised many temperaments that they should marry one woman only.

To permit polygamy does not either mean an interference with the ideal of monogamy, and it certainly need not tend to bring about a decrease in the number of perfectly mated monogamous lives. Among Muslims really monogamous lives are no rarer than among other communities that wish to maintain an appearance of conforming to a more artificial standard of morals. It would not, for instance, be difficult to find Muslim families where the men have been definitely monogamous over a period of four or five generations.

Since the male represents strength and power, his life is not only hazarded in the wars and battles that exist in all ages, but is also risked in the adventurous sports and dangerous occupations of peace. There is, consequently, in all communities a greater loss of life in the male than in the female population. Under this disparity of numbers it is a question how far it is a virtue to enforce a system that robs a large number of women of their natural rights, without leaving them any choice in the matter. If it be a virtue, it none the less means a loss of members to the community. Actually, the average individual does not keep with honesty to such a standard, and so loses the opportunity of procreation without restraining passion. Thus morals are undermined, and prostitution encouraged.

In Afghanistan, which is considered behindhand in progress by the East, but where polygamy, being a natural tendency, is recognized both by law and religion, there are few instances of sexual crime, prostitution is practically unknown, and there are no foundling children.

There are again cases when polygamy from every reasonable point of view seems a necessity; in marriage for instance where the wife is insane, or diseased, or childless. And besides these physical reasons, there are intellectual reasons. Looking into life one sees men unlike in all things. Perhaps one man is equal in his physical strength to ten average men; another is intellectually a giant among his fellows. In Sanskrit *mana* means mind; and the real man is mind. One mind may be equal to a thousand minds. One mind

72

may have innumerable sides, each eager for expression. One mind may be capable of managing innumerable activities, and of supporting innumerable interests.

It was the custom in a country where the people lived by agriculture that each man should receive as his portion a certain plot of land. Some availed themselves of the privilege, and others disregarded their inheritance. Now one man, a good husbandman, saw a field lying untouched and unclaimed, and he passionately desired it; he knew that by his help it could become a fair and beautiful place. And going to the ruler of his country, he demanded of him that field he had thus found lying waste and unclaimed. And the ruler replied, "You are a good husbandman; you have in no wise neglected that which you have; and for myself, I feel grieved that this goodly field that you have seen, should lie overlooked. For it is my desire that my land should be a happy and rich country, and that every part of it should be filled with prosperity. But if I should grant to you this portion, what restraint could I have over other dishonest and neglectful husbandmen? For it is rare to find a man such as yourself. For the most part the husbandmen are slothful and thriftless, thieves and dishonest, scarcely worthy to keep that possession and that liberty which they already have, but ready at all times to snatch at what is not theirs by right." "But", said that good husbandman to the ruler, "if a portion of land remains unclaimed, weeds will grow and all manner of harmful things may breed there; so there is a double loss to your country, for these harmful things spread to other enclosed and cultivated places, and the seeds of the weeds are blown everywhere by the wind." "This I know well", said the ruler of the country, "but it is my duty to make my laws having regard to the worst of my subjects".

It is the lawless, the degenerate, and the mentally incapable who breed and multiply under a system of enforced monogamy; while families that have inherited talent and position are weakened by every kind of artificial restraint, and their unmarried womenfolk in tens of thousands lead artificial lives with natural instincts repressed by conventions of education, law, and religion.

It is not unusual for travellers from the West to comment, with a kind of contempt, upon the swarming poorer populations of Eastern towns. But it will never be easy for Western missionaries to turn the educated Eastern men and women to their views of civilization, once these have seen the teeming streets and slums of European towns, where dirt, disease and drunkenness have so degraded humanity. And not only in the slums of the West does one see violence done to human nature, but there are vast classes whose lives can be called little else but lives of slavery, that are caught and wedged in the wheels of a civilization that crushes and destroys so much beauty of ideal, of personal freedom and expression. Nature is adaptable, and the individual is not always fully conscious of his loss; and therefore not being fully conscious of it, suffers but faintly. The loss of the individual is none the less felt in its entirety by the whole of society. While such things exist under one scheme of civilization, that scheme cannot afford to ignore every other system.

2.

In all ages the thinkers who sought to solve the problem of the universe, have come to the realization

74

that man is the result, and also the aim, of creation. In other words, they have come to the realization that life, the consciousness, which is alone the divine essence, rises upwards from the lowest creation, from the mineral up through the vegetable and animal world, and fulfils its purpose in humanity.

The human creation has therefore been regarded by them as the most sacred creation. The whole tone of Christianity, for example, teaches this. The ideal of the birth of Christ gives an idea of the sacredness of human birth.

The same desire to elevate the ideal of human birth can be seen in every religion; and since religion has at all times held the lives of the people within its grasp, religious customs of various kinds have developed everywhere to surround marriage with sacredness. Because of the idea of the sacredness of human birth, marriage was held sacred. But at the same time polygamy prevailed unrestricted by religion, until the coming of Mohammed.

To see life as a whole is beyond the power of the generality of mankind. The outlook of the average man is bounded by the consideration of the welfare of the race or community to which he happens to belong. In the cycles that form the history of civilization man evolves and degenerates, and often his gain has in the eyes of succeeding generations been seen to be quite outweighed by a corresponding loss. Man sees no further than he sees; and ever and again the turn of the cycle has brought a period of cruelty, of intolerance, and of degeneration.

Krishna has said, "Whenever *dharma* is threatened, then am I born." The Sanskrit word *dharma* has a wider significance than that usually given to 'religion'; it embraces as well the things of Caesar,

as the whole of duty and law. The words of all those
great teachers who have appeared to guide humanity
at different dark moments of history, are of supreme
value; for the very reason that in their vision and
knowledge of life they touched what is beneath and
beyond life, and saw creation as a whole.

It is remarkable that at no time in history was
polygamy restricted by religion until the coming of
Mohammed. He was the first religious teacher to
regulate marriage; until he spoke on the matter,
religion which had always made marriage a sacred
union, had nowhere put any limit to the number of
a man's wives. Christ, Mohammed's great predecessor,
had not pronounced directly or indirectly upon
polygamy, the prevalent custom among the Jews of
the Old Testament.

Looking upon the surface of things many are
tempted to wonder, although few will express the
thought, whether those great teachers of humanity
who themselves led polygamous lives, were actuated
by sensuality, or by some base conception of life and
humanity. Abraham, the father of religion, holy and
pure; Moses, the divinely inspired law-giver; Solomon,
who represents wisdom and justice, — were all these,
whose words are read Sunday by Sunday in services
dedicated to the worship of Christ, besides Krishna,
the Lord of the Hindus, actuated by sensuality or
some base conception of woman?

Digging into their histories we find something very
different. Take for example the life of Mohammed,
who has been so denounced and misunderstood by
the ignorant, although he had a larger number of
followers than any religious teacher. He, with his
broad outlook on life, he, whose actions were prompted
by the highest ideals, had the greatest respect for

76

women as for all humanity. Even in the short oath of allegiance that he exacted from his followers he found a place to show his ideal of woman; for his adherents swore 'to speak no evil of women'. As a young man full of strength and vigour he was the faithful husband of Khatidja; and the proof of his sincerity and faithfulness to her is seen in her unswerving devotion to him. She was the first to believe in his inspired message and to sustain him in it. For the eighteen years of their married life they were everything to each other; she shared with him the dangers and insults of those rigorous years, when to all except to herself and two or three close friends, there seemed no possibility that he should ever succeed in his mission.

How then does this picture of the first part of his life compare with the latter part, after the death of the beloved Khatidja? A great virtue indeed dictated that later conduct of his, which has been so distorted by those who know but little of his teaching. The few who followed Mohammed believed in him to the extent that they lived for him alone; he was to them the representative of God. They sacrificed all, even their lives for him; and he, in his turn, gave them all protection that he could during their lifetime, and supported their widows and children when they died. These women could hardly have returned to their own people, for they were outcasts. Widows of men rejected by their families for giving allegiance to Mohammed, with pride they became members of the household of their Prophet.

Not even the most slanderous of the Prophet's detractors has been able to deny that they lived in happiness and harmony; nor able to prove that he ever dealt except kindly with the women whom he thus took under his care, many of whom were his wives only in name.

Each nation exaggerates the outstanding qualities of the hero it glorifies, and to each the history of the lord and hero of an alien faith, as it is told by its devotees, appears not only incredible, but also repellent. The followers of Mohammed proudly trace relationship with their honoured teacher; thus no doubt this part of his life has been given an unreal prominence, and stories have arisen which have been maliciously perverted by other nationalities and creeds, unable to appreciate their origin. At the same time it is certain that Mohammed in this way brought about reconciliations between enemy tribes, to the great benefit of his people, a fact that his followers have always gratefully recognized. For the orphans and dependents of families that had been divided by ancient jealousies and blood feuds, met together on an equal footing, as honoured members of one family under his protection. Thus he gave to his countrymen a new ideal of patriotism. Hali, the poet of modern Hindustan, the beauty of whose verses and whose ideas of religious and social reform, have evoked the admiration not only of his own countrymen, but also of the Western world, has expressed this fact in a beautiful lyric, which may be thus roughly translated into prose:

He who was truly a merciful teacher,
Who helped the feeble to fulfil their lives,
Who was an ever-present help in sorrow,
Who grieved with his own people and in the trouble of others,
He was my beloved Mohammed.

He who forgave the faults of the wrong-doers,
Who cleansed the hearts of the timorous and despairing from
their fear,
Who vanquished evil with power and with might,
Who reconciled families long at war and embittered against
each other,
He was my beloved Mohammed.

It is not perhaps out of place to cite in this connection that Akbar, the memory of whose reign is engraved upon the hearts of Hindu and Muslim alike, for his wisdom in reconciliating these two faiths, followed in this the example of the Prophet. For, besides the freedom that he gave to his subjects to worship in their own way, whether Christian or Jew, Hindu or Muslim, himself treating the religion of each community not only with sympathy, but also with respect, he chose princesses from different provinces for his wives, and so promoted understanding between followers of different religions, different standards of morals and different customs, that his reign is honoured by all Indians as the most peaceful in the whole history of the Mogul Empire.

It was by quality of mind that the great teachers impressed their messages upon such vast sections of humanity. One mind may be equal to a hundred minds; another to a thousand minds; such is the difference in the quality of men's minds. And it is quality of mind that finds truth, not a quantity of lesser minds. The teaching of any of the great leaders of humanity is of greater value than the opinion that filters through any section of average humanity at any date of history. For the great thinker who contemplates the flow of that divine consciousness which is life, rises in his contemplation above the boundaries which must limit the view of average men, at any and every stage of civilization.

XVII. PERVERSION.

1.

The faculties of intelligence express themselves through physical channels, which they have created for the purpose of their expression. The faculty of sight has created the eyes; that of smell has created the nose; each organ in fact has been developed by a certain faculty, in order to express its particular purpose.

Whichever channel activity works through, it effects some purpose. If rightly directed, it achieves the intended purpose; if wrongly directed, that intended purpose is not accomplished, but some other result is brought about. The ingenuity of science enables the nose to be used as a passage to convey food to the stomach; but science cannot do this without risk of dangerous consequences; and it is a thing quite beyond the unskilled to effect without inflicting injury. To take a railway ticket to Southampton and to wish to go to Southampton, and then to get into a train for Brighton, is called a mistake, or going astray; but those who are in the train for Brighton, wishing to go to Brighton, cannot be said to be going astray. The tracks of the railway line are made for the smooth running of the train; if the train slips off the track, it not only has difficulty in proceeding, but also it causes damage, ploughing up the land and creating destruction in its way.

The generative organs have been developed by the generative faculty; and when used for any other purpose they are misused; any other use directs energy to a wrong channel and creates disorder.

Under a mantle of beauty there may be hidden something desperately evil, while a revolting mask sometimes covers a gem of pure loveliness. The difficulty of touching upon the hideous aspects of life lies in the fact that different social classes are so cut off from one another as to be quite ignorant of each other. Each has its virtues, covering the vices due to its own conventions of life; and to each the vice it does not know appears more intolerable and more unnatural than the vice it is acquainted with.

There is perversion that follows over-indulgence in the beauty that life offers; and equally, perversion follows the too rigid observance of hard and fast moral, social, or religious ideas of order. However beneficial any method of life may appear, it inevitably leads, if carried to excess, to something disastrous or unwholesome which may be called perversion. And so it is that these unwholesome results are usually logical developments of causes of which the individual is the hapless victim; it is not always possible, with justice, to blame him for his condition.

A vast section of civilized society almost ignores the inborn impulses towards beauty and interest; and its unimaginative conception of life weighs not only upon its younger, but grinds also upon its older members. Wherever the natural channels of life are choked and stopped up, other outlets are forced; some of these may seem to be productive of beauty, but most are proved to be eventually productive of innumerable forms of ugliness or cruelty.

Thus the restrictions which some classes place by

their social and religious conventions upon the liberty of the individual, with the laudable motive of preserving standards of order, bring about pitiable situations of life; pitiable as the ruin caused by the lawlessness of those other classes which are too powerful, or too obscure, to submit to restraint.

2.

Music is behind life, and rules life; from music springs all life. The whole creation exists in rhythm. And in a general phrase, it may be said that there is one common source of human disease; and that is disorder in rhythm. Rhythm is broken by congestion; and again rhythm is broken when activity goes beyond the boundaries of normality. For it is a phenomenon of activity that it produces energy of itself. In any activity, in walking, in speaking, in thoughts and imaginations, activity increases with its own energy; so that the speed at the end is greater than the speed at the beginning; until the climax, when it burns itself out. Also activity gains energy, when caught into the speed of a greater activity. Riding quietly along a road one finds that one's horse will break into a canter, if other horses run cantering past.

Perverted desire originates in the debauched, in whom normal desire lives on after physical energy has been spent, and in the physically abnormal and incapable. It originates also in the normal person who is deprived of natural expression. When it arises, the effect is that the normal rhythm of health is broken.

Amongst the former come usually those whose mission in life it is to corrupt others; for just as the spiritually-minded wish to lead others to a spiritual view of life and the materially-minded enjoy life more when they draw others into their circle of gaiety, so also the pervert desires to spread his influence. The perverted have their own groups and recognize each other.

Amongst the latter, that is those in whom natural expression is denied an outlet, are found some who have ideals of life, and who are above all reproach; and their hidden practice may seem quite powerless to break down or injure character, and therefore it may appear quite harmless. But it seems impossible to find any case where health and mind are not affected; for mental despair arises, or confusion, or indecision; or else a physical ailment of a nervous kind; or else a state of mind develops which in its turn produces physical disorder. And here we must reflect that modern science has perhaps still to study the effect of emotion in the blood; this seems to be still a somewhat unexplored field in modern medicine.

The artist stands opposite to nature. It is true that art is nature in miniature; but there is always a tendency in the artist, as he observes nature, to run counter to nature. He observes, and moulds, and creates, and improves, and originates; and thus it is that there is always in him a tendency that leads him out of the natural route of things; therefore it is that perversion is found existing among the followers of art.

But playing with passions and unnatural expression of passion seems to exist in all countries, and at all times; and is never quite uprooted, although it always creates a strong revulsion of feeling.

Creator and creation, — thus goes the natural rhythm of things; nowhere in nature is there room for an intermediary between these two.

They say that ignorance is bliss, but ignorance may well prove to be a curse. There is a tendency in every child that needs guidance, the neglect of which is one of the most fruitful sources of perversion.

This whole subject of perversion in itself is cold and dead; there is no beauty in it; the contemplation of it is deadening, and freezes one. A mother or father turns naturally away to other, creative displays of life and spirit, which have some light and warmth in them, giving an insight into character. For instance, if a child tells a lie, there is as a rule some interest in noticing the type of story that he tells; or perhaps he tells a tale that is in itself thoroughly imaginative and amusing. Also, the innocence of a child is so disarming; and innocence is the surest protective armour against all hurt, a truth every parent knows at heart. But what every parent should recognize is that the intelligence of the child is all the time pushing it to make investigations and experiments that are interesting and new. And it is for the guardian to see that interest receives no unwholesome stimulus. Wherever interest seems strong, it should certainly be disentangled and made straight and clear of mystery in the little mind.

A feeling may be fully awakened in a child before the unperceptive guardian will even think there could be any possibility of the child's having any idea of sex; and a child in its ignorance will deal in its own way with a thing which it finds enjoyable or interesting and will discover some means or other of self-enjoyment. The parents have not spoken to it of such things; and having found some new sensation in life, it gladly seeks a comrade to share in the new interest.

In this way one child learns from another, hiding the fact from his parents; and so a habit may grow and become quite natural, without having any special significance to the child at all.

The impression produced by a habit of this kind has results that are almost incalculable. The abnormal child will no doubt be given a direction that will develop into a definite taste for abnormalities in later years. But the average child will suffer in other ways; it may, for instance, with the years develop a distaste for marriage, or a coldness that affects relationship in marriage. Undeniably, the impression received by its mind will throw some colour on its attitude towards life for many years to come, arousing perhaps a feeling of contempt or of shame for sex; but whatever unhealthy attitude towards nature is thus evoked will affect its whole existence. If parents could realize that every child has an inclination towards perversion which starts as play, and that it needs teaching and guidance in inclination, some to a greater and some to a lesser extent, many disasters might be prevented.

A child is intelligent and can easily be brought to notice the difference between people, and to admire the noble and beautiful; and it can easily be trained to a healthy discrimination with an inclination towards all that is sane, wholesome, and vigorous, as being productive of the greatest happiness and pleasure; and with a contempt of all uncleanliness, and the same fear of the consequences of all unlawfulness. There is no need to punish or to frighten a child, any more than there is any need to feel disgust or fear for a child when it shows an inclination that needs correction, — words usually produce the most remembered impressions.

Children have many influences to deal with that come from without. Not only through other children come unpleasant and perverting suggestions in playtime, — as an English saying goes, "Satan finds some mischief still, for idle hands to do"; but also through older people. Old age often blunts the fineness of feeling; and even among the aged and trusted may be found monstrous tendencies which enjoy watching the spring of interest in the child; ignorant nurses perhaps without thought of harm will play with that interest, and there are monster souls who enjoy above all the thought of being the first to enjoy the passion of youth; and others, who are perhaps of the greatest refinement and delicacy of thought and life and sentiment, who find such an overwhelming attraction in the vigour, in the spring-like beauty of youth, as not to be able to refrain from tampering with it, to get enjoyment and interest out of it in some way or other. Also, there are many older people who have a hatred for the opposite sex which they impart to children. This is especially true of women; and it is not uncommon for women to make a mission of prejudicing young girls against a normal and healthy attitude towards men.

Perhaps there is no grown person who has not a recollection of some occurrence of the sort in his or her own life; but, with a dim memory of the strangeness and horror of it, the grown person remembers too his own extraordinary youthful innocence that came to his rescue; and so he feels inclined to trust to the strength of that same innocence in his own child, not considering in what unknown and difficult position a child may be entangled. Or else a parent may be anxious to protect his girl, and less inclined to protect his boy; never having perhaps traced very carefully what depth of influence that early experience of his, even if of short duration, had on his life; and therefore never having realized what lack of vigour in body, what amount of indecision in mind, of obscurity of purpose, of loss of the total sum of his individual happiness or success might be traced to it. Before the mind of a parent these human tendencies should ever be present; and it is his obligation to awaken in good time the youth under his care.

4.

The knowledge of these things awakens. Not that we are forced thereby to become virtuous; but that we see what power virtue and vice have, looking upon vice as any activity which eventually brings unhappiness to humanity. It is the emotional nature that is susceptible to the desire to experience new sensations; and it is the emotional nature that is the great nature. The great character is on the one side more daring than the average; and on the other more loving, more responsive, more alive, and therefore, more likely to fall into the ditch. But the one who falls, and yet comes out again uninjured, and with wings free and pure, is a rare bird.

There is a temperament that finds it impossible to speak of such subjects, — a temperament that would eagerly desire to warn youth, and to awaken the one who is blindly following a wrong path, but who finds it impossible to speak the necessary words. This reserve springs from a delicate and sensitive respect for human nature; it has been described by Mohammed as *haya*, 'the quality of the truly religious', and prefers to place the greatest trust and confidence in youth, and in friends. It is one that draws out and fosters

87

virtue in others. How many young people owe their unstained records to the trust and confidence placed in them by the mother! At the same time, education requires something more than a silent condemnation; it requires to make clear and understood that law of reciprocity which is the basic law of nature.

An artist relates how his father, whom he greatly respected, gave him no rules of conduct, but treated him always with trust and confidence; and how it was from his brother-in-law, the husband of his much older sister, from whom as a child he learned a much needed warning. The brother-in-law, seeing the ardour, the generosity, the sociability, the enthusiasm for life of the youth, took him to various parts of the town, pointing out the different types of humanity; reminding him at the same time of the great traditions of his race and of his family; of the ideals of his fathers; of the beauty and pride of nobility. What he pointed out and what the youth saw with his own eyes left an undying impression on his mind of the effects of perverted life, influencing the whole trend of his life. Youth is generous, youth is ardent, and rarely fails to respond.

XVIII. PROSTITUTION.

I.

The world looks with contempt on the woman of the street, as a web of evil that drags men's lives to ruin; as a being whose conduct cannot be honourable; as one scarcely worthy of being spoken of. But she gives a welcome to many a one who is quite destitute, or so low or so disagreeable that he could find no other refuge, if refused one by her. The drunken and dissipated men, blind with animal passion; men travelling; strangers in a town and lonely; men who, most strange of all, are advised by a physician to have intercourse with a woman, find a welcome at her door. She is the victim of so much of the evil of the world; she is a martyr, crushed by the refuse of the world. She is, as it were, a human cesspool of the dirt and degradation of society.

Things appear good or bad to the individual according to his own standard, formed usually on his own experiences, good or bad, of life. But it is possible to leave aside one's own standard, — except as a means by which to judge one's self, — and to search for the hidden cause of results. If a man does this, he will find innumerable customs existing for material profit, that are not called prostitution, although there is really no other name for them.

From the earliest times man has bought and sold all things that he needed, and he seldom considers the real value of what he buys, but he fixes a price by the degree of his needs and by his difficulty in satisfying it. For instance, one has seen in wealthy European cities the working-day of workmen and even of children sold for nothing, so that the misery of their conditions cried aloud; and again, at another time they have received a wage, for the same work, that enabled them to lift their heads with some of the dignity that human kind should show; or again, in the other extreme, children have been paid a wage that could have supported a whole family. And these differences in money paid for the same working lives depended on no other fact than the supply of hands in the world of industry. Thus most unnatural customs appear natural to man, who still prides himself with the thought that mankind is ever evolving, and that the latest phase of civilization is the best from all points of view.

And however unnatural it may seem to man, it should be a natural law to him that the least price he can give to a woman in exchange for herself, is his heart; even when he offers to contract marriage with her. If a woman, out of her poverty, willingly sells him her body for money, it is a shame to him if he does not suffice her necessity and help her from principle, and not only from lust.

2.

Harem-zada — son of a harem, — is the lowest word of contempt in the East; its English equivalent could not be printed in an English book. No Eastern lady of position in society, nor any respectable Eastern woman would ever visit a harem; an institution that exists for the pleasure of one rich man, just as in the West, a certain type of chorus girl in theatres and cafés exist for the pleasure of the many. East and West, women show the same unrelenting attitude of sternness towards the prostitute; and one reason is that in all countries women are the main upholders of religion, and no great religion has ever permitted prostitution. But the chief reason of this sternness is undoubtedly the truth, unconsciously known to everyone, that although the human being who has never had an ideal is to be pitied, that one who has had an ideal and has allowed the circumstances of life to break it, has herself thrown away her soul. And it is hard for any woman to tolerate the thought that another woman should be born without an ideal of womanhood.

"The prostitute, grown old, makes a business of her calling, and the girls she has are her slaves", says Sa'adi. Where slavery was banished in its outward appearance in society, prostitution, which is really a slave-business, simply changed hands. The expert prostitute is the centre of this traffic; she not only brings up young girls to it, taking her share of the profits, but to her gravitate the ruined or deserted women, who are too ashamed to go home or who have perhaps none to go to. Before her they feel no shame; and with her welcome, unspoiled by the cold reproaches of hard speech that the virtuous too often proffer with their assistance, she gives kindness and sympathy and also practical help and a means of subsistence.

Only in her springlike youth does the prostitute find anyone to care for her; after that time is passed she often begins to live on the earnings of other women. Sometimes she herself is in the hands of a man who is the real slave-owner of the business;

and at other times she has her men agents who help her to spread her trade for their own profit.

The customs of this trade, which is learned and taught like any other, seem to vary little from country to country; although here and there one finds definite reasons why it should be found flourishing a little more or a little less. When one part of a community is considered entirely subject to another part, or where one race is subject to another in the same country, this business seems to increase. Also military camps have always promoted it; the very conditions of camp life must give scope to it.

Sometimes the human being finds himself in an occupation which works against his conscience; he follows it for the sake of his livelihood only; it satisfies him for a time, because it satisfies his material needs, but there comes a moment in his development when he can bear his yoke no longer. And many times, even in the lives of the most degraded, comes this moment, when they feel that they must grow out of their surroundings, or break away at all costs.

There was once an Indian woman, a singer, who led this degraded life of the prostitute, but she had one quality: when others sang only to please the rich, she would also sing to those who could not pay her. And this generosity in her was the means of leading her to meet and see such souls, as she would have hardly otherwise seen in that profession. At last, the qualities of kindness and charity of heart so developed in her that her voice became an inspiration, and a source of upliftment to many devotional souls. And thus she grew away from her profession; and in the end became renowned for her piety throughout India.

The outlook of the great Teachers whose teachings have changed the outlook upon life of millions and millions in the world, has always been alike in this: they have never been willing to point out the fault in another, and to hurt the faulty one. It was in their regard for the dignity of humanity, in their modesty and service, that lay the beauty and greatness of their great lives.

The mystic voice of Amir has said, "Such beauty lies in Thy forgiveness, that it seems to me that it would have been a sin in me if I had not sinned; for then I should not have known Thy loving-kindness, and the wonder and beauty of Thy true Nature and Being."

Crime is natural. If crime were not natural, from where would it come? All men are subject to fault; their very virtues develop into faults. The great Teacher has therefore taught patience, which means to be patient, and not to expect patience. He has taught respect, which means to show respect, not to demand it. He has taught unselfishness, which means to be unselfish, without expecting a reward. The great Teacher has found his religion in his study of life, and has shown the interdependence of human lives; and that what a man gives, that he receives. He has taught man to lift his light upon high, so that he may live in light; in that light which is never extinguished in man, although usually kept under a covering cloud or a bushel of selfishness and greed, so that its owner lives in a darkened room.

There comes a stage in the moral evolution of man when he perceives and understands the moral of beneficence, and he learns to return good for evil.

93

At this stage in his progress he hears a chord that connects and runs through him and through all. He finds himself as it were a dome, in which good and evil find re-echoing tones. Evil done to him echoes within him in a desire to do evil in return; and good done to him re-echoes in him in a desire to return good. Therefore, in order that his own actions may in their turn call out nothing but good, he desires always to do good; and to return both good for good, and good for evil.

But there is a higher stage to which he may progress; and then it seems to him, that this connecting chord swells into a great sea; and he realizes that the interdependence of lives is such, because the spirit is one; and it is the spirit that unites, and the spirit that gives life.